The
BATHROOM TRIVIA ALMANAC

———— • ————

by

Russ Edwards
and
Jack Kreismer

RED-LETTER PRESS, INC.
Saddle River, New Jersey

THE BATHROOM TRIVIA ALMANAC
REVISED AND UPDATED 2018
COPYRIGHT ©2017 Red-Letter Press, Inc.
ISBN-13: 9781603871532
ISBN: 1603871535

Red-Letter Press, Inc.
P.O. Box 393
Saddle River, NJ 07458

www.Red-LetterPress.com

ACKNOWLEDGMENTS

BOOK DESIGN & TYPOGRAPHY:
Jeff Kreismer

•

COVER ART:
Design by Damonza

•

EDITORIAL:
Jeff Kreismer

•

RESEARCH & DEVELOPMENT:
Kobus Reyneke

The
BATHROOM
TRIVIA
ALMANAC

JANUARY

On This Date: On January 1, 1908, the ball signifying the New Year was dropped for the very first time in New York City's Times Square.

Birthdays: Paul Revere, 1735; Betsy Ross, 1752; J. Edgar Hoover, 1895; Barry Goldwater, 1909; J.D. Salinger, 1919; Frank Langella, 1938; Derrick Thomas, 1967; Morris Chestnut, 1969; Verne Troyer, 1969; Elin Nordegren, 1980

Trivia: Who were Bruce Wayne and Dick Grayson?

Trivia Answer: Batman and Robin, respectively

JANUARY

On This Date: On January 2, 1959, Soviet space probe Luna 1 missed the moon and went into orbit around the sun. All those years we sweated their missiles and these guys missed the MOON!

Birthdays: Isaac Asimov, 1920; Roger Miller, 1936; Jack Hanna, 1947; Cuba Gooding Jr., 1968; Kate Bosworth, 1983

Trivia: Name the three legs, in order of which they are run, of horse racing's Triple Crown.

Trivia Answer: The Kentucky Derby, The Preakness, and The Belmont Stakes

JANUARY

On This Date: On January 3, 1959, Alaska joined Uncle Sam's family, becoming the 49th state of the U.S.

Birthdays: J.R.R. Tolkien, 1892; Victor Borge, 1909; Bobby Hull, 1939; Stephen Stills, 1945; Mel Gibson, 1956; Cheryl Miller, 1964; Eli Manning, 1981

Trivia: If someone called you a blatteroon, should you take it as a compliment?

Trivia Answer: No. A blatteroon talks on and on incessantly, an unfortunate occupational hazard for radio talk show hosts, insurance salesmen and trivia writers.

JANUARY

On This Date: On January 4, 2007, Nancy Pelosi became the first female Speaker of the U.S. House of Representatives.

Birthdays: Sir Isaac Newton, 1643; Jacob Grimm, 1785; Louis Braille, 1809; Tom Thumb, 1838; Don Shula, 1930; Floyd Patterson, 1935; Dyan Cannon, 1937; Kris Bryant, 1992

Trivia: At the age of 76, he was the oldest actor to win the Best Actor Oscar, for his performance in *On Golden Pond*. Name him.

Trivia Answer: Henry Fonda

JANUARY

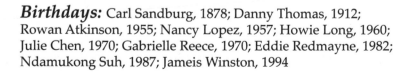

On This Date: On January 5, 1961, TV's *Mr. Ed* debuted. The talking horse would keep on talking for six years.

Birthdays: Stephen Decatur, 1779; Walter Mondale, 1928; Robert Duvall, 1931; Chuck Noll, 1932; Charlie Rose, 1942; Diane Keaton, 1946; Marilyn Manson, 1969; Bradley Cooper, 1975; January Jones, 1978

Trivia: What color nose does Tony the Tiger have?

Trivia Answer: Blue

JANUARY

On This Date: On January 6, 1759, George and Martha Washington were married. Nearly 200 years later, in 1945, George Herbert Walker Bush married Barbara Pierce.

Birthdays: Carl Sandburg, 1878; Danny Thomas, 1912; Rowan Atkinson, 1955; Nancy Lopez, 1957; Howie Long, 1960; Julie Chen, 1970; Gabrielle Reece, 1970; Eddie Redmayne, 1982; Ndamukong Suh, 1987; Jameis Winston, 1994

Trivia: True or false? There has never been a bachelor president in the United States.

Trivia Answer: False – James Buchanan, the 15th president, was unhitched.

JANUARY

On This Date: On January 7, 1972, the Los
Angeles Lakers won their 33rd consecutive game, an
NBA record that still stands today. They would finish the
season with a championship.

Birthdays: Millard Fillmore, 1800; Zora Neale Hurston, 1891;
Kenny Loggins, 1948; Katie Couric, 1957; Rand Paul, 1963;
Nicolas Cage, 1964; Jeremy Renner, 1971; Michael Sam, 1990

Trivia: What Laker ranks as the NBA's all-time leading scorer
with over 38,000 career points?

Trivia Answer: Kareem Abdul-Jabbar

JANUARY

On This Date: On January 8, 1815, the Battle of
New Orleans was fought... two weeks after the war was over!

Birthdays: Soupy Sales, 1926; Elvis Presley, 1935;
Bob Eubanks, 1938; Stephen Hawking, 1942; David Bowie, 1947;
Dwight Clark, 1957; R. Kelly, 1967; Kim Jong-un, 1983

Trivia: Where did the NBA's New Orleans Jazz relocate to in
1979?

Trivia Answer: Salt Lake City, Utah

JANUARY

On This Date: On January 9, 1793, the first successful American balloon flight was made from Philadelphia to New Jersey, piloted by Jean-Pierre Blanchard.

Birthdays: Richard Nixon, 1913; Bart Starr, 1934; Bob Denver, 1935; Dick Enberg, 1935; Joan Baez, 1941; Jimmy Page, 1944; Crystal Gayle, 1951; Dave Matthews, 1967; Chad Johnson, 1978; Kate Middleton, 1982

Trivia: Founder Dave Thomas named this fast food restaurant chain after his daughter, whose real name is Melinda.

Trivia Answer: Wendy's

JANUARY

On This Date: On January 10, 1776, Thomas Paine published *Common Sense*.

Birthdays: Ray Bolger, 1904; Willie McCovey, 1938; Sal Mineo, 1939; Jim Croce, 1943; Rod Stewart, 1945; Linda Lovelace, 1949; George Foreman, 1949; Pat Benatar, 1953

Trivia: What hugely popular book took ten years to write and was the only one ever completed by its author?

Trivia Answer: Gone With The Wind was the famous novel by Margaret Mitchell.

JANUARY 11

On This Date: On January 11, 1987, John Elway led his Broncos on "The Drive", marching 98 yards for a touchdown and ultimately beating the Cleveland Browns in the AFC Championship Game.

Birthdays: Alexander Hamilton, 1755; Clarence Clemons, 1942; Naomi Judd, 1946; Darryl Dawkins, 1957; Mary J. Blige, 1971

Trivia: If you stacked up a pound of one-dollar bills, would there be more or less than 500 of them?

Trivia Answer: Less- A dollar bill weighs one gram and there are 454 grams in a pound.

JANUARY 12

On This Date: On January 12, 1969, the New York Jets made good on Joe Namath's famous guarantee when they shocked the Baltimore Colts, 16-7, in Super Bowl III.

Birthdays: Edmund Burke, 1729; Jack London, 1876; Joe Frazier, 1944; Kirstie Alley, 1951; Rush Limbaugh, 1951; Howard Stern, 1954; Dominique Wilkins, 1960; Jeff Bezos, 1964; Rob Zombie, 1965; Heather Mills, 1968; Zayn Malik, 1993

Trivia: What's odd – or even odder than just plain odd – about the sum of all the numbers on the roulette wheel?

Trivia Answer: They add up to 666 – a number that many attribute to Satan.

JANUARY

On This Date: On January 13, 1966, Lyndon B. Johnson appointed Robert C. Weaver as the first black Cabinet member. Exactly 24 years later, Virginia elected L. Douglas Wilder as the first black governor in the United States.

Birthdays: Robert Stack, 1919; Bob Baffert, 1953; Julia Louis-Dreyfus, 1961; Trace Adkins, 1962; Patrick Dempsey, 1966; Orlando Bloom, 1977; Liam Hemsworth, 1990; Connor McDavid, 1997

Trivia: *The Merry-Go-Round Broke Down* was used as the theme for a long-running cartoon series that is still popular today. Name that 'toon!

Trivia Answer: Looney Tunes

JANUARY

On This Date: On January 14, 1952, *The Today Show* premiered on NBC.

Birthdays: Benedict Arnold, 1741; Albert Schweitzer, 1875; Andy Rooney, 1919; Julian Bond, 1940; Faye Dunaway, 1941; Carl Weathers, 1948; LL Cool J, 1968; Jason Bateman, 1969; Dave Grohl, 1969

Trivia: In 2013, what singer took over for Faith Hill on NBC's *Sunday Night Football* opening?

Trivia Answer: Carrie Underwood

JANUARY 15

On This Date: On January 15, 1967, the Green Bay Packers beat the Kansas City Chiefs, 35-10, in the first game between champions of the NFL and AFL - or Super Bowl I.

Birthdays: Aristotle Onassis, 1906; Martin Luther King, Jr., 1929; Drew Brees, 1979; Pitbull, 1981

Trivia: Do you know the Green Bay Packers quarterback who was the MVP of the first two Super Bowls?

Trivia Answer: Bart Starr

JANUARY 16

On This Date: On January 16, 1973, the first observance of National Nothing Day was held. A day to sit back, relax, and do nothing, it's a much older tradition with Congress.

Birthdays: Ethel Merman, 1908; Roy Jones, Jr., 1969; Kate Moss, 1974; Aaliyah, 1979; Lin-Manuel Miranda, 1980; Albert Pujols, 1980; Joe Flacco, 1985

Trivia: What city is considered to be the undisputed belly dancing capital of the world?

Trivia Answer: Cairo, Egypt

JANUARY

On This Date: On January 17, 1871, Andrew Hallidie was issued a patent for the first cable car.

Birthdays: Benjamin Franklin, 1706; Al Capone, 1899; Betty White, 1922; James Earl Jones, 1931; Shari Lewis, 1933; Maury Povich, 1939; Muhammad Ali, 1942; Andy Kaufman, 1949; Steve Harvey, 1957; Jim Carrey, 1962; Michelle Obama, 1964; Kid Rock, 1971; Zooey Deschanel, 1980; Dwyane Wade, 1982

Trivia: Where is the Great Westminster Clock?

Trivia Answer: In London- Big Ben happens to be the bell inside the tower, not the clock itself.

JANUARY

On This Date: On January 18, 2015, more than six million people attended a Mass in Manila, Philippines, celebrated by Pope Francis.

Birthdays: Peter Mark Roget, 1779; Daniel Webster, 1782; Oliver Hardy, 1892; Cary Grant, 1904; Danny Kaye, 1911; Kevin Costner, 1955; Mark Messier, 1961; Jesse L. Martin, 1969; Jonathan Davis, 1971; Jason Segel, 1980

Trivia: What candy did Clarence Crane introduce in 1912, ironically the same year the Titanic sank?

Trivia Answer: Life Savers

JANUARY 19

On This Date: On January 19, 1974, Notre Dame shocked UCLA to end the Bruins consecutive game winning streak at 88, the longest in NCAA college basketball history.

Birthdays: Robert E. Lee, 1807; Edgar Allan Poe, 1809; Jean Stapleton, 1923; Phil Everly, 1939; Janis Joplin, 1943; Dolly Parton, 1946; Paula Deen, 1947; Katey Sagal, 1954; Junior Seau, 1969; Shawn Wayans, 1971; Jodie Sweetin, 1982; Shawn Johnson, 1992

Trivia: He's the creator of *Jeopardy!*. And the question is, Who is ___?

Trivia Answer: Merv Griffin

JANUARY 20

On This Date: On January 20, 1981, the Iran Hostage Crisis came to a halt with the release of 52 Americans. The release took place just minutes after President Reagan was sworn into office.

Birthdays: George Burns, 1896; Edwin "Buzz" Aldrin, 1930; Bill Maher, 1956; Rainn Wilson, 1966; Questlove, 1971

Trivia: In 1989, Ronald Reagan shared the NBC broadcast booth with Vin Scully during what sport's All-Star Game?

Trivia Answer: Baseball

JANUARY

On This Date: On January 21, 1968, *The Graduate's* film soundtrack was released. It quickly went to #1 on the pop charts and brought Simon & Garfunkel a Grammy for Best Original Score.

Birthdays: Ethan Allen, 1738; Stonewall Jackson, 1824; Benny Hill, 1924; Wolfman Jack, 1938; Jack Nicklaus, 1940; Placido Domingo, 1941; Eric Holder, 1951; Geena Davis, 1956; Hakeem Olajuwon, 1963; Jam Master Jay, 1965

Trivia: What alternative rock band wrote and recorded the theme song for *The Big Bang Theory*?

Trivia Answer: Barenaked Ladies

JANUARY

On This Date: On January 22, 2006, Kobe Bryant scored 81 points in a Lakers win over the Raptors. Bryant's total is second only to Wilt Chamberlain's historic 100-point effort in 1962.

Birthdays: Sam Cooke, 1931; Steve Perry, 1949; DJ Jazzy Jeff, 1965; Diane Lane, 1965; Guy Fieri, 1968; Ray Rice, 1987

Trivia: The opposite sides of a pair of dice always add up to what number?

Trivia Answer: 14 (That's a pair of dice.)

JANUARY

On This Date: On January 23, 1957, the Wham-O toy company produced the first Frisbees.

Birthdays: John Hancock, 1737; Chesley Sullenberger, 1951; Princess Caroline, 1957; Mariska Hargitay, 1964; Julie Foudy, 1971; Tiffani Thiessen, 1974

Trivia: What was the game of Scrabble originally called?

Trivia Answer: Lexico

JANUARY

On This Date: On January 24, 1848, the California Gold Rush began when nuggets were discovered at Sutter's Mill.

Birthdays: Ernest Borgnine, 1917; Neil Diamond, 1941; John Belushi, 1949; Mary Lou Retton, 1968; Matthew Lillard, 1970; Ed Helms, 1974; Mischa Barton, 1986

Trivia: One state in the U.S. is subdivided by "parishes" rather than counties. Which one?

Trivia Answer: Louisiana

JANUARY

On This Date: On January 25, 1924, the very first Winter Olympics began. Chamonix, France had the honor of hosting the Games.

Birthdays: Virginia Woolf, 1882; Etta James, 1938; Eusébio, 1942; Chris Chelios, 1962; Alicia Keys, 1981; Patrick Willis, 1985

Trivia: On a Bingo card, what letter's column contains a free space?

Trivia Answer: N

JANUARY

On This Date: On January 26, 1784, Benjamin Franklin declared that he wanted the turkey, rather than the eagle, as the U.S. symbol.

Birthdays: Douglas MacArthur, 1880; Paul Newman, 1925; Bob Uecker, 1935; Jerry Sandusky, 1944; Gene Siskel, 1946; Eddie Van Halen, 1955; Anita Baker, 1958; Ellen DeGeneres, 1958; Wayne Gretzky, 1961; Vince Carter, 1977; Manti Te'o, 1991

Trivia: In bowling lingo, what is a turkey?

Trivia Answer: A turkey occurs when a person gets three strikes in a row.

JANUARY

On This Date: On January 27, 1880, Thomas Edison got the patent for one of his brightest ideas-the electric light bulb!

Birthdays: Wolfgang Amadeus Mozart, 1756; Lewis Carroll, 1832; Art Rooney, 1901; Mikhail Baryshnikov, 1948; Cris Collinsworth, 1959; Keith Olbermann, 1959

Trivia: What is the highest civilian award in the United States?

Trivia Answer: The Presidential Medal of Freedom

JANUARY

On This Date: On January 28, 1986, the Space Shuttle Challenger exploded barely a minute into its flight, killing all seven crew members aboard.

Birthdays: Jackson Pollock, 1912; Alan Alda, 1936; Gregg Popovich, 1949; Sarah McLachlan, 1968; Rick Ross, 1976; Joey Fatone, 1977; Nick Carter, 1980; Elijah Wood, 1981

Trivia: Originally called "Baby Gays", by what name do we refer to them nowadays?

Trivia Answer: Q-Tips

JANUARY

On This Date: On January 29, 1845, *The Raven,* by Edgar Allan Poe, was published in the *New York Mirror.*

Birthdays: Thomas Paine, 1737; William McKinley, 1843; W. C. Fields, 1880; Tom Selleck, 1945; Oprah Winfrey, 1954; Greg Louganis, 1960; Andre Reed, 1964; Dominik Hasek, 1965; Heather Graham, 1970; Paul Ryan, 1970; Sara Gilbert, 1975; Adam Lambert, 1982

Trivia: What illuminating character did Ryan Reynolds play in the 2011 blockbuster movie that was made after a comic of the same name?

Trivia Answer: The Green Lantern

JANUARY

On This Date: On January 30, 1969, the Beatles played together publicly for the final time on the roof of their Apple Studios. The concert came to an abrupt end when London bobbies broke up the event after neighbors called to complain about the noise. ("You say you want a revolution, well, you know...")

Birthdays: Franklin Delano Roosevelt, 1882; Dick Martin, 1922; Gene Hackman, 1930; Tammy Grimes, 1934; Vanessa Redgrave, 1937; Dick Cheney, 1941; Phil Collins, 1951; Tom Izzo, 1955; Payne Stewart, 1957; Mary Kay Letourneau, 1962; Christian Bale, 1974; Wilmer Valderrama, 1980

Trivia: What presidential daughter had a pony named Macaroni?

Trivia Answer: Caroline Kennedy

JANUARY

On This Date: On January 31, 1958, in response
to the new space race with the Russians, the U.S. launched its
first satellite, Explorer I, an event that lead directly to our
modern world defense, weather and communications satellites.

Birthdays: Tallulah Bankhead, 1902; Jackie Robinson, 1919;
Carol Channing, 1921; Norman Mailer, 1923; Ernie Banks, 1931;
Nolan Ryan, 1947; Minnie Driver, 1970; Portia de Rossi, 1973;
Kerry Washington, 1977; Justin Timberlake, 1981

Trivia: What is the smallest country in the world?

*Trivia Answer: Vatican City- It's recognized as the smallest state in the world, occupying
.2 square miles with a population less than 900.*

FEBRUARY

On This Date: On February 1, 2003, the Space
Shuttle Columbia disintegrated as it tried to re-enter the
Earth's atmosphere after a 16-day mission in space. All seven
members of the crew were lost.

Birthdays: Clark Gable, 1901; Langston Hughes, 1902;
Boris Yeltsin, 1931; Don Everly, 1937; Sherman Hemsley, 1938;
Rick James, 1948; Brandon Lee, 1965; Michelle Akers, 1966;
Lisa Marie Presley, 1968; Pauly Shore, 1968; Michael C. Hall,
1971; Lauren Conrad, 1986; Ronda Rousey, 1987; Harry Styles,
1994

Trivia: William Jonathan Drayton Jr. is known for having a big
timepiece draped around his neck. You know him better by his
stage name. What is it?

Trivia Answer: Flavor Flav

FEBRUARY

On This Date: On February 2, 1887, the first
Groundhog Day was celebrated in Punxsutawney, Pennsylvania.
Ever since then, if meteorological mammal Punxsutawney Phil
comes out of his hole on this day and sees his shadow, it means
six more weeks of winter; no shadow means an early spring.

Birthdays: James Joyce, 1882; George Halas, 1895;
Ayn Rand, 1905; Tom Smothers, 1937; Farrah Fawcett, 1947;
Christie Brinkley, 1954; Shakira, 1977; American Pharoah, 2012

Trivia: What is the southernmost state in the U.S.?

Trivia Answer: Hawaii

FEBRUARY

On This Date: On February 3, 1959, the music
died. Buddy Holly, Richie Valens and J.P. Richardson
(the Big Bopper) perished in an Iowa plane crash. Waylon
Jennings gave up his seat on that ill-fated flight.

Birthdays: Horace Greeley, 1811; Gertrude Stein, 1874;
Norman Rockwell, 1894; James Michener, 1907; Joey Bishop,
1918; Fran Tarkenton, 1940; Blythe Danner, 1943; Bob Griese,
1945; Morgan Fairchild, 1950; Nathan Lane, 1956; Beau Biden,
1969; Amal Alamuddin Clooney, 1978; Julio Jones, 1989;
Sean Kingston, 1990

Trivia: In the January, 1993 issue of *Superman*, the comic book
hero is killed. What enemy is responsible for his death?

Trivia Answer: Doomsday

FEBRUARY 4

On This Date: On February 4, 1974, 19-year-old Patty Hearst was kidnapped by the Symbionese Liberation Army.

Birthdays: Charles Lindbergh, 1902; Byron Nelson, 1912; Rosa Parks, 1913; David Brenner, 1936; Dan Quayle, 1947; Alice Cooper, 1948; Lawrence Taylor, 1959; Oscar De La Hoya, 1973; Natalie Imbruglia, 1975; Gavin DeGraw, 1977; Hannibal Buress, 1983

Trivia: Theodor Geisel is better known by what name?

Trivia Answer: Dr. Seuss

FEBRUARY 5

On This Date: On February 5, 1922, the first edition of *Reader's Digest* was published, a 64-page edition costing a dime. The lead article was written by Alexander Graham Bell on the importance of self-education as a lifelong habit.

Birthdays: Adlai Stevenson, 1900; Red Buttons, 1919; Hank Aaron, 1934; Roger Staubach, 1942; Mark Fuhrman, 1952; Tim Meadows, 1961; Bobby Brown, 1969; Sara Evans, 1971; Cristiano Ronaldo, 1985; Neymar, 1992; Trayvon Martin, 1995

Trivia: Oprah Winfrey, Whoopi Goldberg and Danny Glover were among the cast in this 1985 Steven Spielberg-directed movie about the problems African-American women faced in the early 1900s.

Trivia Answer: The Color Purple

FEBRUARY

On This Date: On February 6, 1971, Alan Shepard became the first person to golf on the moon and the fifth man to walk on it. He would spend a record 33.5 hours on the lunar surface.

Birthdays: Aaron Burr, 1756; Babe Ruth, 1895; Ronald Reagan, 1911; Eva Braun, 1912; Zsa Zsa Gabor, 1917; Tom Brokaw, 1940; Bob Marley, 1945; Natalie Cole, 1950; Axl Rose, 1962; Rick Astley, 1966

Trivia: What Apollo astronaut is the father of a soap star?

Trivia Answer: Michael Collins, left behind to pilot the command module while his shipmates Neil Armstrong and Buzz Aldrin made history by landing on the moon, is the father of Kate Collins, who, for many years, starred on All My Children.

FEBRUARY

On This Date: On February 7, 1964, the British invasion began as those lovable mop tops from Liverpool, The Beatles, landed on U.S. shores.

Birthdays: John Deere, 1804; Charles Dickens, 1812; Sinclair Lewis, 1885; Buster Crabbe, 1908; Emo Philips, 1956; James Spader, 1960; Garth Brooks, 1962; Chris Rock, 1965; Steve Nash, 1974; Ashton Kutcher, 1978; Matthew Stafford, 1988

Trivia: What is the most often-sung tune in the world?

Trivia Answer: "Happy Birthday to You" – The song was composed by sisters Mildred and Patty Hill.

FEBRUARY

On This Date: On February 8, 1910, the Boy
Scouts of America were founded in Chicago.

Birthdays: William Tecumseh Sherman, 1820; Jules Verne,
1828; Lana Turner, 1921; Jack Lemmon, 1925; James Dean, 1931;
John Williams, 1932; Ted Koppel, 1940; Robert Klein, 1942;
Nick Nolte, 1941; John Grisham, 1955; Gary Coleman, 1968;
Alonzo Mourning, 1970; Seth Green, 1974; Bethany Hamilton,
1990; Klay Thompson, 1990

Trivia: Peyton and Eli followed in their father's footsteps as
pro football quarterbacks. What's their pop's first name?

Trivia Answer: Archie (Manning)

FEBRUARY

On This Date: On February 9, 1895, volleyball,
the national pastime of nudist colonies, was invented
by W.G. Morgan of Holyoke, Massachusetts.

Birthdays: William Henry Harrison, 1773; Bill Veeck, 1914;
Carole King, 1942; Joe Pesci, 1943; Mia Farrow, 1945;
Judith Light, 1949; John Kruk, 1961; Travis Tritt, 1963;
Vladimir Guerrero, 1975; Charlie Day, 1976; Michael B. Jordan,
1987

Trivia: What sports Hall of Fame is located in Springfield,
Massachusetts?

Trivia Answer: Basketball

FEBRUARY

On This Date: On February 10, 1897, *The New York Times* introduced its slogan, "All the News That's Fit to Print."

Birthdays: Jimmy Durante, 1893; Robert Wagner, 1930; Mark Spitz, 1950; Greg Norman, 1955; John Calipari, 1959; George Stephanopoulos, 1961; Elizabeth Banks, 1974; Emma Roberts, 1991

Trivia: In Italy, what cheese is often made with water buffalo milk?

Trivia Answer: Mozzarella

FEBRUARY

On This Date: On February 11, 2006, V.P. Dick Cheney accidentally shot Harry Whittington while hunting quail in Texas, thus marking open season on "Duck! It's Dick!" jokes everywhere.

Birthdays: Thomas Edison, 1847; Eva Gabor, 1919; Leslie Nielsen, 1926; Burt Reynolds, 1936; Jeb Bush, 1953; Sheryl Crow, 1962; Sarah Palin, 1964; Jennifer Aniston, 1969; Kelly Slater, 1972; Brandy, 1979; Matthew Lawrence, 1980; Kelly Rowland, 1981; Taylor Lautner, 1992

Trivia: Can you name the only female animal with antlers?

Trivia Answer: A reindeer

FEBRUARY 12

On This Date: On February 12, 2014, a sinkhole estimated at being 30 feet deep and about 40 feet across opened up under the National Corvette Museum in Bowling Green, Kentucky. Eight of the sports cars fell into the sinkhole.

Birthdays: Charles Darwin, 1809; Abraham Lincoln, 1809; General Omar Bradley, 1893; Lorne Greene, 1915; Joe Garagiola, 1926; Bill Russell, 1934; Judy Blume, 1938; Michael McDonald, 1952; Arsenio Hall, 1956, Josh Brolin, 1968; Christina Ricci, 1980; DeMarco Murray, 1988; Robert Griffin III, 1990

Trivia: How many feet deep is a twain?

Trivia Answer: 12

FEBRUARY 13

On This Date: On February 13, 1741, the first American magazine, appropriately titled the *American Magazine*, was published by Andrew Bradford.

Birthdays: Bess Truman, 1885; Tennessee Ernie Ford, 1919; Chuck Yeager, 1923; Stockard Channing, 1944; Jerry Springer, 1944; Mike Krzyzewski, 1947; Peter Gabriel, 1950; Robbie Williams, 1974; Randy Moss, 1977

Trivia: Norman Rockwell illustrated 317 covers over a 47-year period for what magazine?

Trivia Answer: The Saturday Evening Post

FEBRUARY

On This Date: On February 14, 1884, Theodore Roosevelt's two sweethearts, his mother and wife, both died on this Valentine's Day.

Birthdays: Jack Benny, 1894; Jimmy Hoffa, 1913; Mel Allen, 1913; Woody Hayes, 1913; Hugh Downs, 1921; Florence Henderson, 1934; Michael Bloomberg, 1942; Carl Bernstein, 1944; Gregory Hines, 1946; Teller, 1948; Jim Kelly, 1960; Rob Thomas, 1972

Trivia: How many hearts are there on the 6 of hearts?

Trivia Answer: 8

FEBRUARY

On This Date: On February 15, 1903, the first Teddy Bear made its appearance.

Birthdays: Galileo, 1564; Susan B. Anthony, 1820; John Barrymore, 1882; Harvey Korman, 1927; Jane Seymour, 1951; Matt Groening, 1954; Chris Farley, 1964; Jaromir Jagr, 1972; Amy Van Dyken, 1973

Trivia: The first of these fashionable toys was launched in the U.S. dressed in a zebra-style swimsuit in 1959.

Trivia Answer: The Barbie doll

FEBRUARY

On This Date: On February 16, 2005,
Commissioner Gary Bettman canceled the 2004-05
NHL season. This was the first time that a North American
professional sports league canceled an entire season due
to a labor dispute.

Birthdays: Edgar Bergen, 1903; Sonny Bono, 1935;
Kim Jong-il, 1941; LeVar Burton, 1957; John McEnroe, 1959;
Ice-T, 1958; Jerome Bettis, 1972; The Weekend, 1990

Trivia: Name the former Navy SEAL who was a Minnesota
governor and pro wrestler.

Trivia Answer: Jesse Ventura

FEBRUARY

On This Date: On February 17, 2014, American
ice dancing pair Charlie White and Meryl Davis took home the
gold medal during the Sochi Winter Olympics. It was the first
gold ever won by the U.S. in the sport.

Birthdays: Red Barber, 1908; Margaret Truman, 1924;
Hal Holbrook, 1925; Jim Brown, 1936; Michael Jordan, 1963;
Larry the Cable Guy, 1963; Denise Richards, 1971;
Billie Joe Armstrong, 1972; Jerry O'Connell, 1974;
Joseph Gordon-Levitt, 1981; Paris Hilton, 1981; Ed Sheeran, 1991

Trivia: What underwater creature is traditionally thrown onto
the ice during Detroit Red Wings hockey games?

Trivia Answer: Octopus

FEBRUARY

On This Date: On February 18, 1930, Pluto was discovered. He was sitting on a stool at Schwab's when Walt Disney came in… Actually it was the heavenly body Pluto that was discovered (and later "undiscovered" when, in 2006, scientists declared it was not a planet).

Birthdays: Jack Palance, 1919; Helen Gurley Brown, 1922; George Kennedy, 1925; Yoko Ono, 1933; Cybill Shepherd, 1950; John Travolta, 1954; Vanna White, 1957; Matt Dillon, 1964; Dr. Dre, 1965; Molly Ringwald, 1968; Jillian Michaels, 1974; Regina Spektor, 1980; Le'Veon Bell, 1992

Trivia: If you woke up in a state of euneirophrenia, would you scream for your medication or just lay back and enjoy it?

Trivia Answer: Enjoy! It means awakening in a blissful state as if from a pleasant dream.

FEBRUARY

On This Date: On February 19, 1945, World War II's Battle of Iwo Jima began, as nearly 60,000 U.S. Marines stormed the volcanic island.

Birthdays: Nicolaus Copernicus, 1473; Smokey Robinson, 1940; Jeff Daniels, 1955; Roger Goodell, 1959; Seal, 1963; Benicio Del Toro, 1967

Trivia: Where is the Four Corners Monument?

Trivia Answer: It is the quadripoint in the southwestern U.S. where the states of Arizona, Colorado, New Mexico and Utah meet, where visitors can straddle all four states simultaneously.

FEBRUARY

On This Date: On February 20, 1962, Lt. Colonel John Glenn became the first American in orbit as he circled the earth three times in Friendship 7.

Birthdays: Gloria Vanderbilt, 1924; Sidney Poitier, 1927; Bobby Unser, 1934; Nancy Wilson, 1937; Phil Esposito, 1942; Ivana Trump, 1949; Patty Hearst, 1954; Charles Barkley, 1963; Cindy Crawford, 1966; Kurt Cobain, 1967; Justin Verlander, 1983; Trevor Noah, 1984; Rihanna, 1988

Trivia: Which two states have names that come from the Sioux word meaning "friend"?

Trivia Answer: North and South Dakota

FEBRUARY

On This Date: On February 21, 1965, Malcolm X was assassinated. A week after his home was firebombed, the human rights activist was shot to death by Nation of Islam members while speaking at a New York City rally.

Birthdays: Erma Bombeck, 1927; Nina Simone, 1933; Rue McClanahan, 1934; Alan Rickman, 1946; Kelsey Grammer, 1955; Jennifer Love Hewitt, 1979; Jordan Peele, 1979; Ellen Page, 1987; Corbin Bleu, 1989

Trivia: Jacob and Wilhelm were brothers who published short stories under their last name. What was it?

Trivia Answer: Grimm, as in Grimm's Fairy Tales

FEBRUARY

On This Date: On February 22, 1980, the "Miracle on Ice" took place in Lake Placid, NY. The U.S. Olympic hockey team upset the heavily favored Soviets, 4-3, to advance to the finals against Finland.

Birthdays: George Washington, 1732; Connie Mack, 1862; Don Pardo, 1918; Ted Kennedy, 1932; Sparky Anderson, 1934; Robert Kardashian, 1944; Julius Erving, 1950; David Axelrod, 1955; Steve Irwin, 1962; Vijay Singh, 1963; James Blunt, 1974; Drew Barrymore, 1975

Trivia: Who was the first athlete to appear on a Wheaties box?

Trivia Answer: Lou Gehrig, in 1934

FEBRUARY

On This Date: On February 23, 1836 and 1945, the United States lost one and won one - In 1836, the siege of the Alamo began. In 1945, the U.S. flag was raised on Mt. Suribachi on Iwo Jima.

Birthdays: George Frideric Handel, 1685; W.E.B. Du Bois, 1868; Elston Howard, 1929; Peter Fonda, 1939; Ed "Too Tall" Jones, 1951; Daymond John, 1969; Aziz Ansari, 1983; Emily Blunt, 1983; Dakota Fanning, 1994; Andrew Wiggins, 1995

Trivia: Where is the only place the United States flag is flown at full staff 24 hours a day, 365 days a year without ever being raised, lowered, or saluted?

Trivia Answer: The moon

FEBRUARY

On This Date: On February 24, 1868, Andrew Johnson became the first president to be impeached in U.S. history.

Birthdays: Honus Wagner, 1874; Abe Vigoda, 1921; Phil Knight, 1938; Joe Lieberman, 1942; Steve Jobs, 1955; Eddie Murray, 1956; Paula Zahn, 1956; Floyd Mayweather, 1977

Trivia: What man served the shortest term as a U.S. President?

Trivia Answer: William Henry Harrison, who died of pneumonia one month into his term

---

FEBRUARY

On This Date: On February 25, 1964, Muhammad Ali - then Cassius Clay - stunned the boxing world when he captured the heavyweight title over Sonny Liston.

Birthdays: Zeppo Marx, 1901; Jim Backus, 1913; Bob Schieffer, 1937; George Harrison, 1943; Sally Jessy Raphael, 1935; James Brown, 1951; Carrot Top, 1965; Sean Astin, 1971; Chelsea Handler, 1975; Rashida Jones, 1976

Trivia: In 2015, Floyd Mayweather, Jr. fought Manny Pacquiao in one of the most-hyped bouts of all-time. What was the result of the fight?

Trivia Answer: After 12 rounds, Mayweather won by a unanimous decision.

FEBRUARY 26

On This Date: On February 26, 1881, the S.S. Ceylon sailed from Liverpool, England, on the very first around-the-world cruise.

Birthdays: Victor Hugo, 1802; Levi Strauss, 1829; Buffalo Bill Cody, 1846; Grover Cleveland Alexander, 1887; Jackie Gleason, 1916; Tony Randall, 1920; Fats Domino, 1928; Johnny Cash, 1932; Michael Bolton, 1953; Erykah Badu, 1971; Marshall Faulk, 1973

Trivia: If it's 1200 hours in military time, is it noon or midnight?

Trivia Answer: Noon

FEBRUARY 27

On This Date: On February 27, 1883, Oscar Hammerstein obtained a patent for the first cigar rolling machine. By the way, it was Hammerstein who rolled out the lyrics for Richard Rodgers' music.

Birthdays: Henry Wadsworth Longfellow, 1807; Gene Sarazen, 1902; John Steinbeck, 1902; Joanne Woodward, 1930; Elizabeth Taylor, 1932; Ralph Nader, 1934; James Worthy, 1961; Tony Gonzalez, 1976; Chelsea Clinton, 1980; Josh Groban, 1981; Kate Mara, 1983

Trivia: Who is Ted Giannoulas in chicken lore?

Trivia Answer: He's the San Diego Chicken, aka the Famous Chicken, a mascot among mascots, who helped them to become widespread throughout professional sports, particularly Major League Baseball.

FEBRUARY

On This Date: On February 28, 1983, Hawkeye Pierce, B.J. Hunnicutt and the rest of the 4077 struck their tents and hit the road in the final episode of *M*A*S*H*. It registered one of the highest ratings ever as 77 out of 100 people watching TV at the time tuned in.

Birthdays: Linus Pauling, 1901; Bugsy Siegel, 1906; Charles Durning, 1923; Dean Smith, 1931; Mario Andretti, 1940; Bernadette Peters, 1948; Gilbert Gottfried, 1955; John Turturro, 1957; Eric Lindros, 1973; Ali Larter, 1976; Jason Aldean, 1977

Trivia: What does *M*A*S*H* stand for?

Trivia Answer: Mobile Army Surgical Hospital

FEBRUARY

On This Date: On February 29, 2004, *The Lord of the Rings: The Return of the King* won the Best Picture Oscar, along with 10 other awards, at the 76th Annual Academy Awards.

Birthdays: Dinah Shore, 1916; Dennis Farina, 1944; Aileen Wuornos, 1956; Tony Robbins, 1960; Antonio Sabato Jr., 1972; Ja Rule, 1976

Trivia: True or false? There is a town called Leap, Oregon, which was named in a leap year.

Trivia Answer: True

MARCH

On This Date: On March 1, 1972, Texas art teacher Ellen Stanley created National Pig Day, a day to salute our friends, the pigs. So take a pig to lunch; just don't have a pig for lunch!

Birthdays: Frederic Chopin, 1810; Glenn Miller, 1904; Harry Caray, 1914; Pete Rozelle, 1926; Harry Belafonte, 1927; Alan Thicke, 1947; Ron Howard, 1954; Chris Webber, 1973; Mark-Paul Gosselaar, 1974; Lupita Nyong'o, 1983; Kesha, 1987; Justin Bieber, 1994

Trivia: National Pi Day falls on what day of March?

Trivia Answer: 14 – The real "Pi" moments occur March 14, at 1:59 a.m. and p.m. (3.14159...)

MARCH

On This Date: On March 2, 1836, Texas declared its independence from Mexico.

Birthdays: Sam Houston, 1793; Dr. Seuss, 1904; Desi Arnaz, 1917; Mikhail Gorbachev, 1931; Lou Reed, 1942; Karen Carpenter, 1950; Jon Bon Jovi, 1962; Daniel Craig, 1968; Chris Martin, 1977; Rebel Wilson, 1980; Bryce Dallas Howard, 1981; Ben Roethlisberger, 1982; Reggie Bush, 1985

Trivia: Ernest Evans' biggest hit record was *The Twist*. You know him better by his weight-related nickname. What is it?

Trivia Answer: Chubby Checker

MARCH

On This Date: On March 3, 1887, Helen Keller met her "miracle worker", Anne Sullivan, who arrived at the Keller household to work with the six-year-old.

Birthdays: Alexander Graham Bell, 1847; Perry Ellis, 1940; Jackie Joyner-Kersee, 1962; Herschel Walker, 1962; Julie Bowen, 1970; Jessica Biel, 1982

Trivia: George Wendt, who played Norm on *Cheers*, is the uncle of what former *Saturday Night Live* cast member?

Trivia Answer: Jason Sudeikis (Wendt is his mother's brother.)

MARCH

On This Date: On March 4, 1952, Ronald Reagan married Nancy Davis.

Birthdays: Knute Rockne, 1888; Rick Perry, 1950; Catherine O'Hara, 1954; Patricia Heaton, 1958; Chaz Bono, 1969; Landon Donovan, 1982; Bobbi Kristina Brown, 1993

Trivia: What TV husband and wife lived at 623 East 68th Street in Manhattan?

Trivia Answer: I Love Lucy's Ricky and Lucy Ricardo

MARCH

On This Date: On March 5, 1963, the Hula-Hoop was patented by the Wham-O company's co-founder, Arthur "Spud" Melin.

Birthdays: Penn Jillette, 1955; Andy Gibb, 1958; Joel Osteen, 1963; Michael Irvin, 1966; Eva Mendes, 1974; Niki Taylor, 1975

Trivia: How many squares are there on each side of a Rubik's cube?

Trivia Answer: 9

MARCH

On This Date: On March 6, 1930, Clarence Birdseye put the first individually packaged frozen foods on sale.

Birthdays: Michelangelo, 1475; Cyrano de Bergerac, 1619; Elizabeth Barrett Browning, 1806; Lou Costello, 1906; Ed McMahon, 1923; Alan Greenspan, 1926; Gabriel Garcia Marquez, 1927; Valentina Tereshkova, 1937; Willie Stargell, 1940; Rob Reiner, 1947; Tom Arnold, 1959; D.L. Hughley, 1963; Connie Britton, 1967; Shaquille O'Neal, 1972

Trivia: Can you name the oldest fast-food hamburger chain?

Trivia Answer: White Castle, which opened in 1921

MARCH

On This Date: On March 7, 2010, Kathryn Bigelow became the first female director to win an Oscar.

Birthdays: Willard Scott, 1934; Michael Eisner, 1942; Franco Harris, 1950; Lynn Swann, 1952; Bryan Cranston, 1956; Wanda Sykes, 1964; Jenna Fischer, 1974

Trivia: Who was Margaret Herrick and what unique place does she hold in the history of the Academy Awards?

Trivia Answer: She was a secretary who happened to remark that the new statuette looked like her Uncle Oscar. The name stuck. Years later, she became the excecutive director of the academy.

MARCH

On This Date: On March 8, 1894, bureaucracy caught up to man's best friend as New York City passed its first dog licensing law.

Birthdays: Alan Hale, Jr., 1921; Jim Rice, 1953; Lester Holt, 1959; Freddie Prinze, Jr., 1976; Hines Ward, 1976; James Van Der Beek, 1977

Trivia: How many teeth does a typical dog have: 22, 32 or 42?

Trivia Answer: 42 – 20 on top and 22 on the lower jaw

MARCH

On This Date: On March 9, 1996, legendary comedian George Burns died at 100. His death came just weeks after celebrating his milestone birthday.

Birthdays: Amerigo Vespucci, 1454; Yuri Gagarin, 1934; Bobby Fischer, 1943; Kato Kaelin, 1959; Steve Wilkos, 1964; Clint Dempsey, 1983; Shad "Bow Wow" Moss, 1987

Trivia: What comedian was the first host of *Saturday Night Live* in October of 1975?

Trivia Answer: George Carlin

MARCH

On This Date: On March 10, 1876, Alexander Graham Bell transmitted the very first telephone call to his assistant, Mr. Watson.

Birthdays: Chuck Norris, 1940; Jim Valvano, 1946; Osama bin Laden, 1957; Sharon Stone, 1958; Rod Woodson, 1965; Jon Hamm, 1971; Timbaland, 1972; Shannon Miller, 1977; Robin Thicke, 1977; Carrie Underwood, 1983; Olivia Wilde, 1984

Trivia: What is the American "911" emergency telephone number equivalent in Great Britain?

Trivia Answer: 999

MARCH

On This Date: On March 11, 1302, according to William Shakespeare, Romeo Montague and Juliet Capulet were married by Friar Laurence.

Birthdays: Lawrence Welk, 1903; Rupert Murdoch, 1931; Sam Donaldson, 1934; Antonin Scalia, 1936; Terrence Howard, 1969; Johnny Knoxville, 1971; Anthony Davis, 1993

Trivia: What is the only food that doesn't spoil?

Trivia Answer: Honey

MARCH

On This Date: On March 12, 1912, Juliette Low earned some big-time brownie points as she organized the first Girl Scout troop in Savannah, Georgia.

Birthdays: Jack Kerouac, 1922; Liza Minnelli, 1946; Mitt Romney, 1947; James Taylor, 1948; Darryl Strawberry, 1962; Aaron Eckhart, 1968

Trivia: What sports "first" belongs to Diane Crump?

Trivia Answer: Diane Crump was the first female (human, anyway) to participate in the Kentucky Derby.

MARCH

On This Date: On March 13, 2013, Jorge Mario Bergoglio, aka Pope Francis, was elected as the 266th Roman Catholic pontiff.

Birthdays: L. Ron Hubbard, 1911; Neil Sedaka, 1939; William H. Macy, 1950; Common, 1972; Emile Hirsch, 1985; Mikaela Shiffrin, 1995

Trivia: What's the national flower of the United States?

Trivia Answer: Rose

MARCH

On This Date: On March 14, 1923, Warren G. Harding became the first president to file an income tax.

Birthdays: Albert Einstein, 1879; Michael Caine, 1933; Quincy Jones, 1933; Billy Crystal, 1948; Kirby Puckett, 1960; Stephen Curry, 1988; Simone Biles, 1997

Trivia: This major and historic city is named after President Polk's vice-president.

Trivia Answer: Dallas

MARCH

15

On This Date: On March 15, 44 B.C., Julius
Caesar was told to "beware the Ides of March." He must
not have kept his ides open, as he was assassinated.

Birthdays: Andrew Jackson, 1767; Ruth Bader Ginsburg,
1933; Mike Love, 1941; Sly Stone, 1944; Fabio, 1959;
Bret Michaels, 1963; Mark McGrath, 1968; Mike Tomlin, 1972;
Eva Longoria, 1975; will.i.am, 1975

Trivia: Which common household pet possesses a Jacobson's
organ?

Trivia Answer: A cat - The Jacobson's organ is a scent organ in the roof of a cat's mouth.

MARCH

16

On This Date: On March 16, 1802, West Point
Military Academy in New York was established by an
Act of Congress.

Birthdays: James Madison, 1751; Pat Nixon, 1912;
Jerry Lewis, 1926; Daniel Patrick Moynihan, 1927;
Chuck Woolery, 1941; Erik Estrada, 1949; Flavor Flav, 1959;
Lauren Graham, 1967; Brooke Burns, 1978; Blake Griffin, 1989

Trivia: Riverdale High's Kevin is the first character in the long
history of Archie comic books to be _____.

Trivia Answer: Gay

MARCH

On This Date: On March 17, 1766, the first recorded St. Patrick's Day Parade was held in New York City. In Maryville, Missouri, they'll be out in less than full force again today, as each year they break their own record for the shortest St. Paddy's Parade.

Birthdays: Bobby Jones, 1902; Nat King Cole, 1919; Patrick Duffy, 1949; Kurt Russell, 1951; Gary Sinise, 1955; Dana Reeve, 1961; Rob Lowe, 1964; Mia Hamm, 1972

Trivia: Lucky the Leprechaun is the mascot of what NBA franchise?

Trivia Answer: Boston Celtics

MARCH

On This Date: On March 18, 1931, the electric razor was first marketed by Schick.

Birthdays: Grover Cleveland, 1837; George Plimpton, 1927; John Updike, 1932; Vanessa Williams, 1963; Bonnie Blair, 1964; Andre Rison, 1967; Queen Latifah, 1970; Dane Cook, 1972; Adam Levine, 1979

Trivia: What television network made its debut on January 1, 2011, replacing the Discovery Health Channel?

Trivia Answer: OWN- The Oprah Winfrey Network

MARCH

On This Date: On March 19, 1931, we bet you didn't know that Nevada legalized gambling.

Birthdays: Wyatt Earp, 1848; William Jennings Bryan, 1860; Earl Warren, 1891; Glenn Close, 1947; Harvey Weinstein, 1952; Bruce Willis, 1955; Andy Reid, 1958; Clayton Kershaw, 1988

Trivia: This Internet service was founded in 1983 as the Control Video Corporation (CVC).

Trivia Answer: AOL

MARCH

On This Date: On March 20, 1852, *Uncle Tom's Cabin*, by Harriet Beecher Stowe, was published.

Birthdays: Carl Reiner, 1922; Fred Rogers, 1928; Pat Riley, 1945; Bobby Orr, 1948; Spike Lee, 1957; Holly Hunter, 1958; Kathy Ireland, 1963

Trivia: What whale of a story begins with "Call me Ishmael"?

Trivia Answer: Moby Dick

MARCH

On This Date: On March 21, 1891, a Hatfield and a McCoy were married, ending a lengthy West Virginia feud. Watch for them on the next episode of *Family Feud*!

Birthdays: Timothy Dalton, 1946; Eddie Money, 1949; Gary Oldman, 1958; Matthew Broderick, 1962; Rosie O'Donnell, 1962; Kevin Federline, 1978; Ronaldinho, 1980; Adrian Peterson, 1985

Trivia: How many years of marriage are celebrated on a Crystal Anniversary?

Trivia Answer: 15

MARCH

On This Date: On March 22, 1882, the Edmunds Act was passed. Signed into law by president Chester A. Arthur, it declared polygamy a felony.

Birthdays: Chico Marx, 1887; Karl Malden, 1912; Marcel Marceau, 1923; Pat Robertson, 1930; Stephen Sondheim, 1930; William Shatner, 1931; George Benson, 1943; James Patterson, 1947; Wolf Blitzer, 1948; Andrew Lloyd Webber, 1948; Bob Costas, 1952; Keegan-Michael Key, 1971; Reese Witherspoon, 1976; J.J. Watt, 1989

Trivia: The last name is Buonarroti. What's the first name?

Trivia Answer: Michelangelo

MARCH

On This Date: On March 23, 1775, Patrick Henry gave his "Give Me Liberty or Give Me Death" speech. Henry was a happy man... eventually he got both.

Birthdays: Joan Crawford, 1905; Roger Bannister, 1929; Chaka Khan, 1953; Geno Auriemma, 1954; Moses Malone, 1955; Catherine Keener, 1959; Jason Kidd, 1973; Keri Russell, 1976; Perez Hilton, 1978; Brandon Marshall, 1984; Kyrie Irving, 1992

Trivia: What is the oldest college in the U.S.?

Trivia Answer: Harvard University, established in 1636

MARCH

On This Date: On March 24, 1958, Elvis got his sideburns chopped and his head shaved as he gave a two-year command performance for Uncle Sam.

Birthdays: Harry Houdini, 1874; Fatty Arbuckle, 1887; Steve McQueen, 1930; Tommy Hilfiger, 1951; Louie Anderson, 1953; Star Jones, 1962; Lara Flynn Boyle, 1970; Jim Parsons, 1973; Alyson Hannigan, 1974; Peyton Manning, 1976; Chris Bosh, 1984

Trivia: There are two common colors which have no words that rhyme with them. One is purple. What's the other?

Trivia Answer: Orange

MARCH

On This Date: On March 25, 1954, RCA began production of the first commercial color TV sets, equipped with a 15-inch picture tube.

Birthdays: Howard Cosell, 1918; Gloria Steinem, 1934; Anita Bryant, 1940; Aretha Franklin, 1942; Elton John, 1947; Marcia Cross, 1962; Sarah Jessica Parker, 1965; Sheryl Swoopes, 1971; Danica Patrick, 1982; Katharine McPhee, 1984; Ryan Lewis, 1988

Trivia: Who holds the record for appearing on the cover of *TV Guide* the most times?

Trivia Answer: Lucille Ball, with over 30 appearances

MARCH

On This Date: On March 26, 1953, Dr. Jonas Salk announced a new vaccine to immunize against polio.

Birthdays: Robert Frost, 1874; Tennessee Williams, 1911; Sandra Day O'Connor, 1930; Leonard Nimoy, 1931; Alan Arkin, 1934; Harry Kalas, 1936; James Caan, 1940; Nancy Pelosi, 1940; Bob Woodward, 1943; Diana Ross, 1944; Steven Tyler, 1948; Vicki Lawrence, 1949; Martin Short, 1950; Leeza Gibbons, 1957; Marcus Allen, 1960; Jennifer Grey, 1960; John Stockton, 1962; Kenny Chesney, 1968; Leslie Mann, 1972; Keira Knightley, 1985; Von Miller, 1989

Trivia: Dr. Benjamin Spock, American child care guru, achieved quite a distinction in sports in his youth. Any idea what it was?

Trivia Answer: Strangely enough, the great opponent of paddling was a member of the American rowing gold medal team in the 1924 Olympics.

MARCH

On This Date: On March 27, 1998, the Food and Drug Administration approved the use of a drug of great impotence...er, importance - Viagra.

Birthdays: Gloria Swanson, 1899; Cale Yarborough, 1939; Randall Cunningham, 1963; Quentin Tarantino, 1963; Mariah Carey, 1970; Fergie, 1975; Buster Posey, 1987; Jessie J, 1988; Matt Harvey, 1989

Trivia: What's the name of the rooster on the Kellogg's Corn Flakes box?

Trivia Answer: Cornelius

MARCH

On This Date: On March 28, 1384, King Richard II condemned the consumption of cats. Ever since then, it's been called Respect Your Cat Day.

Birthdays: Rick Barry, 1944; Reba McEntire, 1955; Vince Vaughn, 1970; Kate Gosselin, 1975; Julia Stiles, 1981; Lady Gaga, 1986

Trivia: What is the largest cat on earth?

Trivia Answer: A tiger

MARCH

On This Date: On March 29, 2004, The Republic of Ireland became the first country in the world to ban smoking in all workplaces, including bars and restaurants.

Birthdays: John Tyler, 1790; Cy Young, 1867; Sam Walton, 1918; Pearl Bailey, 1918; Walt Frazier, 1945; Earl Campbell, 1955; Elle Macpherson, 1964; Lucy Lawless, 1968; Jennifer Capriati, 1976

Trivia: What Disney dog was originally called Rover?

Trivia Answer: Pluto

MARCH

On This Date: On March 30, 1981, John Hinckley Jr. shot and wounded President Ronald Reagan in Washington, D.C.

Birthdays: Vincent van Gogh, 1853; Warren Beatty, 1937; Eric Clapton, 1945; Paul Reiser, 1957; MC Hammer, 1962; Tracy Chapman, 1964; Ian Ziering, 1964; Piers Morgan, 1965; Celine Dion, 1968; Secretariat, 1970; Norah Jones, 1979; Richard Sherman, 1988

Trivia: In 1997, Bill Clinton underwent surgery to repair an injured knee that he suffered outside the house of what golfer?

Trivia Answer: Greg Norman

MARCH

On This Date: On March 31, 1889, the Eiffel
Tower opened for business in Paris.

Birthdays: Rene Descartes, 1596; Johann Sebastian Bach, 1685;
Cesar Chavez, 1927; Gordie Howe, 1928; Liz Claiborne, 1929;
Herb Alpert, 1935; Barney Frank, 1940; Christopher Walken,
1943; Al Gore, 1948; Rhea Perlman, 1948; Ewan McGregor, 1971

Trivia: What's located at 350 Fifth Avenue, New York, New
York?

Trivia Answer: The Empire State Building

APRIL

On This Date: On April 1, 1996, the Taco Bell
corporation announced that it had bought the Liberty
Bell and was renaming it the Taco Liberty Bell.

Birthdays: Debbie Reynolds, 1932; Ali MacGraw, 1939;
Phil Niekro, 1939; Susan Boyle, 1961; Rachel Maddow, 1973

Trivia: What is Bell's phenomenon?

*Trivia Answer: When eye muscles relax and the eyes roll back above their usual position,
such as when we're asleep*

APRIL

On This Date: On April 2, 1792, Congress established the United States Mint in Philadelphia.

Birthdays: Charlemagne, 742; Hans Christian Andersen, 1805; Buddy Ebsen, 1908; Marvin Gaye, 1939; Emmylou Harris, 1947; Rodney King, 1965; Bill Romanowski, 1966

Trivia: As you look at it, which way does the eagle's head face on the flip side of a quarter?

Trivia Answer: Left

APRIL

On This Date: On April 3, 1860, the first Pony Express began. It hightailed between Sacramento, California, and St. Joseph, Missouri.

Birthdays: Washington Irving, 1783; Marlon Brando, 1924; Doris Day, 1924; Wayne Newton, 1942; Tony Orlando, 1944; Alec Baldwin, 1958; Eddie Murphy, 1961; Jennie Garth, 1972; Adam Scott, 1973; Leona Lewis, 1985; Amanda Bynes, 1986

Trivia: He won the popular vote, but finished second in the electoral vote and thus lost the presidential race to George W. Bush in 2000.

Trivia Answer: Al Gore

APRIL

On This Date: On April 4, 1968, Martin Luther King, Jr. was assassinated in Memphis, Tennessee, by James Earl Ray.

Birthdays: Muddy Waters, 1915; Gil Hodges, 1924; Maya Angelou, 1928; Clive Davis, 1932; Anthony Perkins, 1932; Craig T. Nelson, 1944; Robert Downey Jr., 1965; David Blaine, 1973; Heath Ledger, 1979; Jamie Lynn Spears, 1991

Trivia: What does ROY G. BIV stand for?

Trivia Answer: It is a common acronym to help remember the order of the colors of the rainbow- red, orange, yellow, green, blue, indigo and violet.

APRIL

On This Date: On April 5, 1614, John Rolfe and Pocahontas were married in Virginia.

Birthdays: Booker T. Washington, 1856; Glenn "Pop" Warner, 1871; Spencer Tracy, 1900; Bette Davis, 1908; Gregory Peck, 1916; Frank Gorshin, 1933; Colin Powell, 1937; Michael Moriarty, 1941; Pharrell Williams, 1973

Trivia: What dog was the first animal to be named to the Animal Hall of Fame in 1969?

Trivia Answer: Lassie

APRIL 6

On This Date: On April 6, 1896, the first modern Olympic Games began in Athens, Greece.

Birthdays: Merle Haggard, 1937; Billy Dee Williams, 1937; John Ratzenberger, 1947; Marilu Henner, 1952; Michele Bachmann, 1956; Sterling Sharpe, 1965; Paul Rudd, 1969; Zach Braff, 1975; Candace Cameron Bure, 1976

Trivia: If you are dining in England and order broccoli, what will you get?

Trivia Answer: Cauliflower

APRIL 7

On This Date: On April 7, 1967, Roger Ebert wrote his very first film review for the *Chicago Sun-Times*. The movie? *Galia.*

Birthdays: Billie Holiday, 1915; James Garner, 1928; Francis Ford Coppola, 1939; David Frost, 1939; John Oates, 1949; Jackie Chan, 1954; Tony Dorsett, 1954; Christopher Darden, 1956; Russell Crowe, 1964; Bill Bellamy, 1965; Ronde & Tiki Barber, 1975; Danny Almonte, 1987

Trivia: What gum's distinctive flavor comes from vanilla, wintergreen and a form of cinnamon called cassia?

Trivia Answer: Bubble gum

APRIL

On This Date: On April 8, 1974, Hank Aaron hit career home run #715, breaking the all-time record held by Babe Ruth. Aaron clouted another 40 homers before retiring.

Birthdays: Sonja Henie, 1912; Betty Ford, 1918; Kofi Annan, 1938; John Havlicek, 1940; Catfish Hunter, 1946; Robert L. Johnson, 1946; Gary Carter, 1954; Patricia Arquette, 1968; Chris Kyle, 1974; Felix Hernandez, 1986

Trivia: What "first" do baseball luminaries Babe Ruth, Sparky Anderson and Tom Seaver share?

Trivia Answer: The same first name – George

APRIL

On This Date: On April 9, 1965, the first indoor baseball game was played at the Astrodome in Houston, Texas. The Astros defeated the New York Yankees, 2-1, in an exhibition contest.

Birthdays: Curly Lambeau, 1898; Hugh Hefner, 1926; Dennis Quaid, 1954; Cynthia Nixon, 1966; Jenna Jameson, 1974; Kristen Stewart, 1990; Elle Fanning, 1998

Trivia: What was the name of the second baseman in Abbott and Costello's "Who's on First?" routine.

Trivia Answer: That's right. Look at the quiz and you'll note that it's a statement, not a question.

APRIL

On This Date: On April 10, 1849, Walter Hunt invented the safety pin and traded his patent for a safety net - he got 100 bucks for it.

Birthdays: Joseph Pulitzer, 1847; Chuck Connors, 1921; Omar Sharif, 1932; John Madden, 1936; Don Meredith, 1938; Steven Seagal, 1952; Babyface, 1959; Mandy Moore, 1984; Haley Joel Osment, 1988

Trivia: Several decades ago, George de Mestral took a walk in the woods. Afterwards, the cockleburs he noticed sticking to his clothing became his inspiration for what invention?

Trivia Answer: Velcro

APRIL

On This Date: On April 11, 1970, NASA launched Apollo 13. Two days later, an explosion on the spacecraft's moon landing mission forced the astronauts to abandon the mission and return to Earth.

Birthdays: Ethel Kennedy, 1928; Joel Grey, 1932; Mark Teixeira, 1980; Joss Stone, 1987

Trivia: True or false? Napoleon Bonaparte designed the flag of Italy.

Trivia Answer: True

APRIL

On This Date: On April 12, 1861, Confederates fired on Fort Sumter in Charleston Harbor, touching off the Civil War.

Birthdays: Henry Clay, 1777; Beverly Cleary, 1916; Tiny Tim, 1932; Herbie Hancock, 1940; Robert Durst, 1943; Ed O'Neill, 1946; Tom Clancy, 1947; David Letterman, 1947; David Cassidy, 1950; Andy Garcia, 1956; Vince Gill, 1957; Shannen Doherty, 1971; Claire Danes, 1979; Jessie James Decker, 1988

Trivia: During the Civil War, were there any slave states that remained part of the Union?

Trivia Answer: Yes – They were Delaware, Kentucky, Maryland and Missouri.

APRIL

On This Date: On April 13, 2016, in his final NBA game, Kobe Bryant dropped 60 points in a Lakers win over the Jazz. That same night, the Golden State Warriors won their 73rd game of the season, passing the 1995-96 Chicago Bulls in the record books.

Birthdays: Thomas Jefferson, 1743; Butch Cassidy, 1866; Don Adams, 1923; Tony Dow, 1945; Al Green, 1946; Max Weinberg, 1951; Garry Kasparov, 1963; Caroline Rhea, 1964; Allison Williams, 1988

Trivia: If you were gambrinous, would you be more likely to go to the bedroom, the kitchen, the bathroom or the laundry room?

Trivia Answer: As it means full of beer, hopefully you would choose the bathroom before any of the others.

APRIL

14

On This Date: On April 14, 1865, President Lincoln was shot by John Wilkes Booth at Ford's Theater in Washington, D.C.

Birthdays: Anne Sullivan, 1866; Rod Steiger, 1925; Loretta Lynn, 1932; Julie Christie, 1940; Pete Rose, 1941; Brad Garrett, 1960; Greg Maddux, 1966; Anthony Michael Hall, 1968; Adrien Brody, 1973; Sarah Michelle Gellar, 1977; Abigail Breslin, 1996

Trivia: What fateful contact did the Lincoln family have with the Booth family prior to 1865?

Trivia Answer: In one of the strangest coincidences in history, one day in Jersey City a young Robert Todd Lincoln, Abe's son, fell between railroad cars and was rescued by actor Edwin Booth, brother of John Wilkes Booth.

APRIL

15

On This Date: On April 15, 1955, Ray Kroc opened his first McDonald's restaurant. The slogan at the time was "Q.S.C.V." (Quality, Service, Cleanliness and Value).

Birthdays: Leonardo da Vinci, 1452; Nikita Khrushchev, 1894; Elizabeth Montgomery, 1933; Dodi Fayed, 1955; Evelyn Ashford, 1957; Emma Thompson, 1959; Dara Torres, 1967; Jason Sehorn, 1971; Chris Stapleton, 1978; Seth Rogen, 1982; Emma Watson, 1990

Trivia: Ronald McDonald is the real name of the character portrayed by Rob McElhenney on what sitcom?

Trivia Answer: It's Always Sunny in Philadelphia

APRIL

On This Date: On April 16, 1940, Cleveland's
Bob Feller threw the only Opening Day no-hitter in
Major League Baseball history.

Birthdays: Wilbur Wright, 1867; Charlie Chaplin, 1889;
Peter Ustinov, 1921; Henry Mancini, 1924; Pope Benedict XVI,
1927; Bobby Vinton, 1935; Kareem Abdul-Jabbar, 1947;
Bill Belichick, 1952; Ellen Barkin, 1954; Jon Cryer, 1965;
Martin Lawrence, 1965; Selena, 1971; Akon, 1973

Trivia: What's the most amount of change you could have
without being able to make change for a dollar bill?

Trivia Answer: $1.19- Three quarters, four dimes and four pennies

APRIL

On This Date: On April 17, 1961, an invasion
force halfheartedly backed by the United States was
repelled at Cuba's Bay of Pigs.

Birthdays: J.P. Morgan, 1837; William Holden, 1918;
Harry Reasoner, 1923; Sean Bean, 1959; Boomer Esiason, 1961;
Jennifer Garner, 1972; Victoria Beckham, 1974; Rooney Mara,
1985

Trivia: What school did the Delta frats attend in *Animal House*?

Trivia Answer: Faber College

APRIL

On This Date: On April 18, 1775, Paul Revere went on his legendary midnight ride to warn the countryside that "The British are coming!" Along with Revere rode William Dawes, who never got credit despite the fact that Revere was captured early on, had his horse taken away from him and was sent packing back to Boston on foot, leaving Dawes to alert the patriots.

Birthdays: Clarence Darrow, 1857; James Woods, 1947; Rick Moranis, 1953; Jeff Dunham, 1962; Eric McCormack, 1963; Conan O'Brien, 1963; Melissa Joan Hart, 1976; Miguel Cabrera, 1983; America Ferrera, 1984

Trivia: What do the Roman Numerals MDCCLXXVI stand for?

Trivia Answer: 1776 (That's the spirit!)

APRIL

On This Date: On April 19, 1995, a truck bomb exploded outside the Alfred P. Murrah Federal Building in Oklahoma City, killing 168 people and injuring 500. Timothy McVeigh was convicted of the bombing and sentenced to death.

Birthdays: Jayne Mansfield, 1933; Dudley Moore, 1935; Tim Curry, 1946; Suge Knight, 1965; Ashley Judd, 1968; James Franco, 1978; Kate Hudson, 1979; Hayden Christensen, 1981; Troy Polamalu, 1981; Candace Parker, 1986; Maria Sharapova, 1987

Trivia: How many nines are there between 1 and 100?

Trivia Answer: 20

APRIL

20

On This Date: On April 20, 1986, Michael Jordan set an NBA postseason record with 63 points against the Boston Celtics. His Bulls, however, lost to the Celtics in double overtime.

Birthdays: Adolf Hitler, 1889; Lionel Hampton, 1908; Tito Puente, 1923; George Takei, 1937; Ryan O'Neal, 1941; Steve Spurrier, 1945; Jessica Lange, 1949; Luther Vandross, 1951; Don Mattingly, 1961; Carmen Electra, 1972; Joey Lawrence, 1976; Luke Kuechly, 1991

Trivia: In 2016, who smashed his own NBA record when he hit 402 three-pointers during the season?

Trivia Answer: Stephen Curry

APRIL

21

On This Date: On April 21, 1980, Rosie Ruiz came out of nowhere to win the Boston Marathon. A post-race investigation revealed that was just what she did. Ruiz was disqualified for not running the entire course and Jacqueline Gareau of Canada was declared the winner.

Birthdays: Queen Elizabeth II, 1926; Charles Grodin, 1935; Iggy Pop, 1947; Gary Condit, 1948; Tony Danza, 1951; Rob Riggle, 1970; Tony Romo, 1980

Trivia: What is the largest city in both Maine and in Oregon?

Trivia Answer: Portland

APRIL

On This Date: On April 22, 1864, the phrase "In God We Trust" was first added to United States coinage. One previous slogan printed on earlier coins was "Mind Your Business".

Birthdays: Immanuel Kant, 1724; Nikolai Lenin, 1870; J. Robert Oppenheimer, 1904; Glen Campbell, 1936; Jack Nicholson, 1937; Peter Frampton, 1950; Ryan Stiles, 1959; Sherri Shepherd, 1967; Marshawn Lynch, 1986

Trivia: What was the largest denomination of United States currency ever minted?

Trivia Answer: A $100,000 bill, which bore a portrait of Woodrow Wilson

---

APRIL

On This Date: On April 23, 1985, New Coke was introduced. Sales increased, but acceptance of the taste fizzed, err fizzled, so Coca-Cola went back to the old formula.

Birthdays: William Shakespeare, 1564; James Buchanan, 1791; Stephen A. Douglas, 1813; Warren Spahn, 1921; Shirley Temple, 1928; Roy Orbison, 1936; Michael Moore, 1954; Valerie Bertinelli, 1960; George Lopez, 1961; Timothy McVeigh, 1968; John Cena, 1977; John Oliver, 1977; Kal Penn, 1977

Trivia: How many bones are there in the human body?

Trivia Answer: 206

APRIL

On This Date: On April 24, 1888, Kodak sold its
first camera.

Birthdays: Shirley MacLaine, 1934; Sue Grafton, 1940;
Barbra Streisand, 1942; Cedric the Entertainer, 1964;
Chipper Jones, 1972; Carlos Beltran, 1977; Kelly Clarkson, 1982

Trivia: Eric Blair wrote *Animal Farm* and *Nineteen Eighty-Four.*
What is his more common pen name?

Trivia Answer: George Orwell

APRIL

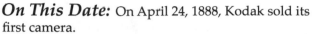

On This Date: On April 25, 1901, New York
became the first state to require license plates on cars.

Birthdays: Oliver Cromwell, 1599; Guglielmo Marconi, 1874;
Edward R. Murrow, 1908; Ella Fitzgerald, 1917; Al Pacino, 1940;
Adam Silver, 1962; Joe Buck, 1969; Renee Zellweger, 1969;
Jason Lee, 1970; Tim Duncan, 1976

Trivia: You've probably got to be a Baby Boomer to get this
one. What was the theme song of the cowboy TV program
The Roy Rogers Show?

Trivia Answer: Happy Trails

APRIL

On This Date: On April 26, 1986, the Chernobyl nuclear power plant exploded.

Birthdays: John James Audubon, 1785; Carol Burnett, 1933; Bobby Rydell, 1942; Jet Li, 1963; Kevin James, 1965; Melania Trump, 1970; Channing Tatum, 1980; Aaron Judge, 1992

Trivia: Popeye is perpetually how old?

Trivia Answer: 34

APRIL

On This Date: On April 27, 2011, President Barack Obama produced a detailed Hawaii birth certificate to demonstrate proof of U.S. citizenship when he was born.

Birthdays: Samuel Morse, 1791; Ulysses S. Grant, 1822; Rogers Hornsby, 1896; Jack Klugman, 1922; Coretta Scott King, 1927; Casey Kasem, 1932; George Gervin, 1952; Sheena Easton, 1959; Cory Booker, 1969

Trivia: What's the most popular first name for a U.S. president?

Trivia Answer: James (Madison, Monroe, Polk, Buchanan, Garfield, and Carter)

APRIL

28

On This Date: On April 28, 1966, the Boston Celtics won their eighth consecutive NBA title, beating the Los Angeles Lakers in Game 7, 95-93.

Birthdays: James Monroe, 1758; Lionel Barrymore, 1878; Harper Lee, 1926; Saddam Hussein, 1937; Ann-Margret, 1941; Jay Leno, 1950; Barry Larkin, 1964; John Daly, 1966; Bridget Moynahan, 1971; Penelope Cruz, 1974; Jessica Alba, 1981

Trivia: What is the first name of TV's Dr. Oz?

Trivia Answer: Mehmet

APRIL

29

On This Date: On April 29, 1913, Gideon Sundback of Hoboken, New Jersey, received a patent for the zipper.

Birthdays: William Randolph Hearst, 1863; Duke Ellington, 1899; Emperor Hirohito, 1901; Rod McKuen, 1933; Willie Nelson, 1933; Bernie Madoff, 1938; Dale Earnhardt, 1951; Jerry Seinfeld, 1954; Kate Mulgrew, 1955; Daniel Day-Lewis, 1957; Michelle Pfeiffer, 1958; Andre Agassi, 1970; Uma Thurman, 1970; Jay Cutler, 1983

Trivia: What does "ZIP", as in zip code, stand for?

Trivia Answer: Zone Improvement Plan

APRIL

On This Date: On April 30, 1939, Franklin Delano Roosevelt became the first U.S. president to appear on television during the World Fair's opening ceremonies broadcast.

Birthdays: Cloris Leachman, 1926; Isiah Thomas, 1961; Johnny Galecki, 1975; Kunal Nayyar, 1981; Kirsten Dunst, 1982

Trivia: What Allstate Insurance spokesman played U.S. President David Palmer in the hit Fox series *24*?

Trivia Answer: Dennis Haysbert

MAY

On This Date: On May 1, 1931, the Empire State Building opened.

Birthdays: Calamity Jane, 1852; Kate Smith, 1907; Glenn Ford, 1916; Jack Paar, 1918; Judy Collins, 1939; Rita Coolidge, 1945; Tim McGraw, 1967; Curtis Martin, 1973; Wes Welker, 1981; Jamie Dornan, 1982

Trivia: Do you know the only word in the English language which ends in "sede"?

Trivia Answer: Supersede

MAY

On This Date: On May 2, 1885, the first issue of *Good Housekeeping* cleaned up at the newsstands.

Birthdays: Catherine the Great, 1729; Dr. Benjamin Spock, 1903; Engelbert Humperdinck, 1936; Christine Baranski, 1952; Dwayne "The Rock" Johnson, 1972; David Beckham, 1975; Kyle Busch, 1985; Paul George, 1990; Princess Charlotte, 2015

Trivia: When *Rolling Stone* premiered back in 1967, what familiar face graced the cover of the first issue?

Trivia Answer: John Lennon

MAY

On This Date: On May 3, 1973, construction was completed on Chicago's Sears Tower, making it the tallest building in the U.S.

Birthdays: Niccolo Machiavelli, 1469; Bing Crosby, 1903; Sugar Ray Robinson, 1921; James Brown, 1933; Frankie Valli, 1934; Greg Gumbel, 1946; Levi Johnston, 1990

Trivia: The tallest man in the world was Robert Wadlow, who died at the age of 22 in 1940. Was he over or under nine feet?

Trivia Answer: Under – 8'11"

MAY

On This Date: On May 4, 1970, at Kent State in Ohio, National Guardsmen fired their rifles into a group of students protesting the Vietnam War, killing four and injuring several others.

Birthdays: Hosni Mubarak, 1928; Audrey Hepburn, 1929; Jackie Jackson, 1951; Randy Travis, 1959; Will Arnett, 1970; Erin Andrews, 1978; Lance Bass, 1979; Rory McIlroy, 1989

Trivia: This 007 star was the oldest ever to win *People Magazine's* "Sexiest Man Alive" award. Who is he?

Trivia Answer: Sean Connery, 59, in 1989

MAY

On This Date: On May 5, 1961, Commander Alan B. Shepard, Jr. sat atop a Redstone booster at Cape Canaveral and became the first American in space with his brief sub-orbital flight.

Birthdays: Karl Marx, 1818; Tammy Wynette, 1942; Brian Williams, 1959; Henry Cavill, 1983; Adele, 1988; Brooke Hogan, 1988; Chris Brown, 1989

Trivia: If your musical tastes were corybantic, would you more likely attend the symphony or a rock concert?

Trivia Answer: A rock concert- Corybantic means wild and frenzied.

MAY

On This Date: On May 6, 1954, Roger Bannister became the first man to run the mile in less than four minutes. The British student broke the tape in 3:59.4.

Birthdays: Sigmund Freud, 1856; Robert E. Peary, 1856; Rudolph Valentino, 1895; Orson Welles, 1915; Willie Mays, 1931; Bob Seger, 1945; Tony Blair, 1953; Tom Bergeron, 1955; George Clooney, 1961; Martin Brodeur, 1972; Jason Witten, 1982; Gabourey Sidibe, 1983; Chris Paul, 1985; Meek Mill, 1987; Jose Altuve, 1990

Trivia: What former president's face is on the $2 bill?

Trivia Answer: Thomas Jefferson

MAY

On This Date: On May 7, 1915, the Lusitania sank after being torpedoed by a German U-boat, hastening American involvement in World War I.

Birthdays: Gary Cooper, 1901; Darren McGavin, 1922; Johnny Unitas, 1933; Tim Russert, 1950; Owen Hart, 1965; Breckin Meyer, 1974

Trivia: Before you turn in for the night, you'll probably pandiculate a time or two. What will you be doing?

Trivia Answer: Yawning

MAY

On This Date: On May 8, 1886, Dr. John Pemberton of Atlanta, Georgia, invented Coca-Cola.

Birthdays: Harry S. Truman, 1884; Don Rickles, 1926; Sonny Liston, 1932; Ricky Nelson, 1940; Toni Tennille, 1940; Bill Cowher, 1957; Ronnie Lott, 1959; Bill de Blasio, 1961; Melissa Gilbert, 1964; Enrique Iglesias, 1975

Trivia: *You Got the Right One, Baby* was a popular Diet Pepsi jingle that featured what musician in its commercials?

Trivia Answer: Ray Charles

MAY

On This Date: On May 9, 1950, L. Ron Hubbard's book *Dianetics: The Modern Science of Mental Health* was published, a landmark moment in the history of Scientology.

Birthdays: Mike Wallace, 1918; Candice Bergen, 1946; Billy Joel, 1949; Tony Gwynn, 1960; Steve Yzerman, 1965; Rosario Dawson, 1979

Trivia: Who was the originator of the military decoration known as "The Purple Heart"?

Trivia Answer: George Washington

MAY

On This Date: On May 10, 1869, the Golden Spike was driven in Promontory, Utah, to complete the first transcontinental railroad.

Birthdays: John Wilkes Booth, 1838; Fred Astaire, 1899; Pat Summerall, 1930; Donovan, 1946; Chris Berman, 1955; Mark David Chapman, 1955; Sid Vicious, 1957; Rick Santorum, 1958; Bono, 1960; Kenan Thompson, 1978; Missy Franklin, 1995

Trivia: If you give a hoot about *Harry Potter* films and know who's who, you probably know Hedwig. What relationship has he with Harry?

Trivia Answer: He's Potter's pet owl.

MAY

On This Date: On May 11, 1987, the first ever heart-lung transplant took place in Baltimore, Maryland. The surgery was performed by Dr. Bruce Reitz of Stanford University School of Medicine.

Birthdays: Irving Berlin, 1888; Salvador Dali, 1904; Natasha Richardson, 1963; Cory Monteith, 1982; Cam Newton, 1989

Trivia: Just like its predecessor *Breaking Bad, Better Call Saul* is set and produced in what location?

Trivia Answer: Albuquerque, New Mexico

MAY

On This Date: On May 12, 1932, the infant son
of Charles Lindbergh, ten weeks after being abducted, was
found dead in Hopewell, New Jersey, just a few miles from
the Lindberghs' home.

Birthdays: Florence Nightingale, 1820; Katharine Hepburn,
1907; Yogi Berra, 1925; Burt Bacharach, 1928; George Carlin, 1937;
Emilio Estevez, 1962; Stephen Baldwin, 1966; Tony Hawk, 1968;
Kim Fields, 1969; Jason Biggs, 1978

Trivia: When the first Hummer was sold to the public, what
celebrity bought it?

Trivia Answer: Arnold Schwarzenegger

MAY

On This Date: On May 13, 1981, Pope John Paul
II was shot and seriously wounded by Turkish assailant
Mehmet Ali Agca in St. Peter's Square.

Birthdays: Joe Louis, 1914; Bea Arthur, 1922; Harvey Keitel,
1939; Stevie Wonder, 1950; John Kasich, 1952; Dennis Rodman,
1961; Stephen Colbert, 1964; Darius Rucker, 1966; Lena Dunham,
1986; Robert Pattinson, 1986

Trivia: Who created Garfield in 1978?

Trivia Answer: Jim Davis

MAY

On This Date: On May 14, 1853, Gail Borden
applied for a U.S. patent for his process for making
condensed milk. His process turned out to be a cash cow as it
was eventually marketed by a company, no coincidence here,
called Borden.

Birthdays: Bobby Darin, 1936; George Lucas, 1944;
Cate Blanchett, 1969; Roy Halladay, 1977; Mark Zuckerberg,
1984; Rob Gronkowski, 1989; Miranda Cosgrove, 1993

Trivia: Where did Nike get its name?

Trivia Answer: From the Greek Goddess of Victory

MAY

On This Date: On May 15, 1930, Ellen Church,
the first "air hostess", greeted passengers aboard a flight
between California and Chicago.

Birthdays: Madeleine Albright, 1937; Trini Lopez, 1937;
Kathleen Sebelius, 1948; George Brett, 1953; Dan Patrick, 1956;
Emmitt Smith, 1969; Desmond Howard, 1970; Ray Lewis, 1975;
Jamie-Lynn Sigler, 1981; Andy Murray, 1987

Trivia: What breed of dog starred in the *Beethoven* film series?

Trivia Answer: Saint Bernard

MAY

16

On This Date: On May 16, 1929, the first Oscars were given out. The silent film *Wings* won Best Picture.

Birthdays: Henry Fonda, 1905; Liberace, 1919; Billy Martin, 1928; Pierce Brosnan, 1953; Olga Korbut, 1955; Joan Benoit, 1957; Janet Jackson, 1966; Thurman Thomas, 1966; Tracey Gold, 1969; Tori Spelling, 1973; Megan Fox, 1986

Trivia: If you saw Virginia Katherine McMath and Frederick Austerlitz in a movie, what would they most likely be doing?

Trivia Answer: Dancing – They were Ginger Rogers and Fred Astaire.

MAY

17

On This Date: On May 17, 1875, Aristides was the winner of the first Kentucky Derby at Churchill Downs in Louisville.

Birthdays: James "Cool Papa" Bell, 1903; Dennis Hopper, 1936; Bill Paxton, 1955; Sugar Ray Leonard, 1956; Bob Saget, 1956; Jim Nantz, 1959; Enya, 1961; Craig Ferguson, 1962; Jordan Knight, 1970; Tony Parker, 1982; Matt Ryan, 1985

Trivia: Javier Colon was the winner of the inaugural season of what reality TV show?

Trivia Answer: The Voice

MAY 18

On This Date: On May 18, 1980, Mt. St. Helens erupted in the state of Washington, leaving 57 people dead.

Birthdays: Perry Como, 1912; Pope John Paul II, 1920; Brooks Robinson, 1937; Reggie Jackson, 1946; George Strait, 1952; Tina Fey, 1970; Jack Johnson, 1975

Trivia: What baseball team plays their home games at 1060 West Addison Street in Chicago?

Trivia Answer: The Cubs- It's the address of Wrigley Field.

MAY 19

On This Date: On May 19, 1911, the long arm of the law first used fingerprints to get a conviction.

Birthdays: Johns Hopkins, 1795; Ho Chi Minh, 1890; Malcolm X, 1925; Nora Ephron, 1941; Pete Townshend, 1945; Andre the Giant, 1946; Archie Manning, 1949; Nicole Brown Simpson, 1959; Kevin Garnett, 1976; Sam Smith, 1992

Trivia: The popular catchphrase "How sweet it is!" was first said by what comedian?

Trivia Answer: Jackie Gleason

MAY

On This Date: On May 20, 1927, "Lucky Lindy," Charles Augustus Lindbergh, began his successful solo flight across the Atlantic.

Birthdays: Dolley Madison, 1768; James Stewart, 1908; Joe Cocker, 1944; Cher, 1946; Cindy McCain, 1954; Timothy Olyphant, 1968; Busta Rhymes, 1972

Trivia: EWR, LAX, DFW, and ORD are abbreviations for what airports?

Trivia Answer: EWR is Newark Airport; LAX is Los Angeles; DFW is Dallas-Fort Worth; and ORD is for O'Hare in Chicago (from the old Orchard Field).

MAY

On This Date: On May 21, 1881, Clara Barton founded the American Red Cross in Washington, D.C.

Birthdays: Raymond Burr, 1917; Al Franken, 1951; Mr. T, 1952; Judge Reinhold, 1957; Jeffrey Dahmer, 1960; Chris Benoit, 1967; The Notorious B.I.G, 1972; Ricky Williams, 1977; Gotye, 1980; Josh Hamilton, 1981

Trivia: You'd have to be lucky and lead a charmed life to have a chance at finding some marbits. Where are they?

Trivia Answer: Look in a box of Lucky Charms cereal. Those are the little bits of marshmallow inside.

MAY

On This Date: On May 22, 1992, it was "Therrrre Goes Johnny!" After a reign that spanned the Cuban Missile Crisis, Woodstock, Watergate, disco, Reagan and the Gulf War, Johnny Carson retired from *The Tonight Show*.

Birthdays: Arthur Conan Doyle, 1859; Laurence Olivier, 1907; Harvey Milk, 1930; Ted Kaczynski, 1942; Mike Breen, 1961; Naomi Campbell, 1970; Apolo Anton Ohno, 1982; Novak Djokovic, 1987

Trivia: What group has been Jimmy Fallon's house band since 2009, when he first started on late night TV?

Trivia Answer: The Roots

MAY

On This Date: On May 23, 1785, Ben Franklin was old enough to need bifocals, so he invented them.

Birthdays: Ambrose Burnside, 1824; Joan Collins, 1933; Marvelous Marvin Hagler, 1954; Drew Carey, 1958; Ken Jennings, 1974; Jewel, 1974; Kelly Monaco, 1976

Trivia: Lazy Susans are named after what inventor's daughter?

Trivia Answer: Thomas Edison

MAY

24

On This Date: On May 24, 1935, President
Franklin Delano Roosevelt pressed a button at the White
House that turned on the lights for Major League Baseball's
first night game, at Crosley Field in Cincinnati.

Birthdays: Tommy Chong, 1938; Bob Dylan, 1941;
Patti LaBelle, 1944; Priscilla Presley, 1945; John C. Reilly, 1965;
Tracy McGrady, 1979; Billy Gilman, 1988

Trivia: What is the only eight-letter word in the English
language with only one vowel?

Trivia Answer: Strength

MAY

25

On This Date: On May 25, 1968, the Gateway
Arch in St. Louis formally opened.

Birthdays: Ralph Waldo Emerson, 1803; Bill "Bojangles"
Robinson, 1878; Ian McKellen, 1939; Mike Myers, 1963;
Anne Heche, 1969; Jamie Kennedy, 1970; Brian Urlacher, 1978

Trivia: Name the diminutive actor who played Tattoo on
television's *Fantasy Island.*

Trivia Answer: Herve Villechaize

MAY

On This Date: On May 26, 1978, Atlantic City became the first city outside Nevada to offer legalized casino gambling.

Birthdays: Al Jolson, 1886; John Wayne, 1907; Miles Davis, 1926; Jack Kevorkian, 1928; Brent Musburger, 1939; Stevie Nicks, 1948; Hank Williams Jr., 1949; Sally Ride, 1951; Lenny Kravitz, 1964; Helena Bonham Carter, 1966; Matt Stone, 1971; Lauryn Hill, 1975

Trivia: What was Mario's original name in The Super Mario Brothers video game?

Trivia Answer: Jumpman

MAY

On This Date: On May 27, 1937, the Golden Gate Bridge in San Francisco opened.

Birthdays: Wild Bill Hickok, 1837; Hubert Humphrey, 1911; Sam Snead, 1912; Henry Kissinger, 1923; Jeff Bagwell, 1968; Frank Thomas, 1968; Lisa "Left Eye" Lopes, 1971; Andre 3000, 1975; Jamie Oliver, 1975

Trivia: What four faces did Gutzon Borglum sculpt?

Trivia Answer: The four presidential faces of Mt. Rushmore: George Washington, Abraham Lincoln, Thomas Jefferson and Theodore Roosevelt

MAY

On This Date: On May 28, 1957, NL owners
allowed the Brooklyn Dodgers and New York Giants to move
to California, leaving the Big Apple without National League
baseball until the Mets came to town in 1962.

Birthdays: Jim Thorpe, 1888; Jerry West, 1938; Rudolph
Giuliani, 1944; Gladys Knight, 1944; John Fogerty, 1945;
Kylie Minogue, 1968; Rob Ford, 1969; Marco Rubio, 1971;
Elisabeth Hasselbeck, 1977; Colbie Caillat, 1985; Michael Oher,
1986

Trivia: Wayne Gretzky is the NHL's all-time leading scorer.
Who's second?

Trivia Answer: Mark Messier (Gretzky scored 2,857 points, Messier 1,887.)

MAY

On This Date: On May 29, 1953, Sir Edmund
Hillary and Tenzing Norgay became the first men to
reach the summit of Mount Everest.

Birthdays: Patrick Henry, 1736; Bob Hope, 1903; John F.
Kennedy, 1917; Al Unser, 1939; La Toya Jackson, 1956; Annette
Bening, 1958; Melissa Etheridge, 1961; Melanie Brown, 1975;
Daniel Tosh, 1975; Carmelo Anthony, 1984

Trivia: Steve Fossett completed a "first of its kind" trip around
the world in 2002. By what method did he travel?

Trivia Answer: In a balloon- It took him 14 days, 19 hours and 51 minutes.

MAY

On This Date: On May 30, 1911, Ray Harroun won the first Indianapolis 500 with a blistering average speed of 74.6 miles per hour.

Birthdays: Mel Blanc, 1908; Benny Goodman, 1909; Gale Sayers, 1943; Wynonna Judd, 1964; Idina Menzel, 1971; Manny Ramirez, 1972; Cee Lo Green, 1974

Trivia: What beverage does the winner of the Indianapolis 500 traditionally drink?

Trivia Answer: Milk

MAY

On This Date: On May 31, 1927, the last Ford Model T rolled off the assembly line after a production run of 15,007,003 vehicles.

Birthdays: Walt Whitman, 1819; Fred Allen, 1894; Norman Vincent Peale, 1898; Don Ameche, 1908; Clint Eastwood, 1930; Peter Yarrow, 1938; Joe Namath, 1943; Tom Berenger, 1949; Lea Thompson, 1961; Brooke Shields, 1965; Colin Farrell, 1976

Trivia: Which state has the most miles of highway and the most vehicles per square mile?

Trivia Answer: The Garden State, New Jersey

JUNE

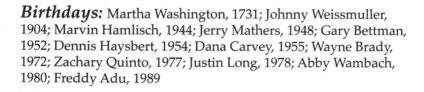

On This Date: On June 1, 1980, CNN made its debut as the world's first 24-hour television news network.

Birthdays: Brigham Young, 1801; Andy Griffith, 1926; Marilyn Monroe, 1926; Pat Boone, 1934; Morgan Freeman, 1937; Alexi Lalas, 1970; Heidi Klum, 1973; Alanis Morissette, 1974; Amy Schumer, 1981; Justine Henin, 1982

Trivia: Who was married to Auntie Em in *The Wizard of Oz*?

Trivia Answer: Uncle Henry

JUNE

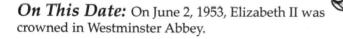

On This Date: On June 2, 1953, Elizabeth II was crowned in Westminster Abbey.

Birthdays: Martha Washington, 1731; Johnny Weissmuller, 1904; Marvin Hamlisch, 1944; Jerry Mathers, 1948; Gary Bettman, 1952; Dennis Haysbert, 1954; Dana Carvey, 1955; Wayne Brady, 1972; Zachary Quinto, 1977; Justin Long, 1978; Abby Wambach, 1980; Freddy Adu, 1989

Trivia: Did America ever have a King for president?

Trivia Answer: Yes – Former President Gerald R. Ford was born Leslie King.

JUNE

On This Date: On June 3, 1888, *The San Francisco Examiner* published *Casey at the Bat*, a poem written by Ernest Lawrence Thayer.

Birthdays: Jefferson Davis, 1808; Tony Curtis, 1925; Raul Castro, 1931; Anderson Cooper, 1967; Rafael Nadal, 1986

Trivia: In *Casey at the Bat*, what team was Casey playing for?

Trivia Answer: The Mudville Nine

JUNE

On This Date: On June 4, 1896, Henry Ford drove the Quadricycle, his very first automobile, onto the streets of Detroit, where he made it several blocks before breaking down.

Birthdays: Dr. Ruth Westheimer, 1928; Russell Brand, 1975; Angelina Jolie, 1975; Bar Refaeli, 1985

Trivia: Quick - which travels farther on a bike - the front wheel or back wheel?

Trivia Answer: It's the front wheel, which moves back and forth as the bike is steered while the back wheel travels in a straight path.

JUNE

On This Date: On June 5, 1968, Robert F. Kennedy was assassinated by Sirhan Sirhan just after claiming victory in California's Democratic presidential primary.

Birthdays: Pancho Villa, 1878; Bill Moyers, 1934; Suze Orman, 1951; Kenny G, 1956; Brian McKnight, 1969; Mark Wahlberg, 1971; Pete Wentz, 1979

Trivia: What was Frosty the Snowman's nose made from?

Trivia Answer: A button

JUNE

On This Date: On June 6, 1944, Allied troops stormed ashore at Normandy Beach for D-Day, Operation Overload.

Birthdays: Nathan Hale, 1755; Robert Englund, 1947; Harvey Fierstein, 1954; Bjorn Borg, 1956; Paul Giamatti, 1967; Natalie Morales, 1972

Trivia: What is the "D" in D-Day an abbreviation for?

Trivia Answer: It simply stands for "Day" to reiterate its military importance.

JUNE

On This Date: On June 7, 1982, Priscilla Presley opened Elvis's home, Graceland, to the public. The bathroom where Elvis died five years earlier would be kept off-limits.

Birthdays: Dean Martin, 1917; Tom Jones, 1940; Thurman Munson, 1947; Liam Neeson, 1952; L.A. Reid, 1956; Prince, 1958; Dave Navarro, 1967; Allen Iverson, 1975; Bill Hader, 1978; Anna Kournikova, 1981; Michael Cera, 1988; Iggy Azalea, 1990

Trivia: If a baseball player has earned the golden sombrero, what has he done?

Trivia Answer: He has struck out four times in one game.

JUNE

On This Date: On June 8, 1869, the housekeeper's friend, I.W. McGaffey, received his patent for the first vacuum cleaner.

Birthdays: Frank Lloyd Wright, 1867; Byron "Whizzer" White, 1917; Barbara Bush, 1925; Jerry Stiller, 1927; Joan Rivers, 1933; Nancy Sinatra, 1940; Bonnie Tyler, 1951; Keenen Ivory Wayans, 1958; Julianna Margulies, 1966; Gabrielle Giffords, 1970; Lindsay Davenport, 1976; Kanye West, 1977; Maria Menounos, 1978; Kim Clijsters, 1983

Trivia: What does TMZ stand for?

Trivia Answer: Thirty Mile Zone (which represents an area that lies in a 30 mile radius of the intersection of West Beverly Blvd. and North La Cienega Blvd. in Los Angeles)

JUNE

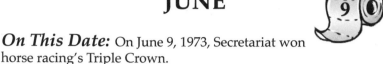

On This Date: On June 9, 1973, Secretariat won horse racing's Triple Crown.

Birthdays: Cole Porter, 1891; Les Paul, 1915; Jackie Mason, 1931; Dick Vitale, 1939; Michael J. Fox, 1961; Aaron Sorkin, 1961; Johnny Depp, 1963; Natalie Portman, 1981

Trivia: Only two mammals lay eggs rather than give birth to live offspring. Name them.

Trivia Answer: The duck-billed platypus and the spiny anteater

---

JUNE

On This Date: On June 10, 2007, the final episode of *The Sopranos*, ranked by *TV Guide* as the best television series of all time, aired on HBO.

Birthdays: Prince Philip, 1921; Judy Garland, 1922; Maurice Sendak, 1928; F. Lee Bailey, 1933; Dan Fouts, 1951; John Edwards, 1953; Eliot Spitzer, 1959; Elizabeth Hurley, 1965; Bobby Jindal, 1971; Tara Lipinski, 1982; Kate Upton, 1992

Trivia: What TV personality had been nominated for over 30 Emmys before finally winning for the first time in 2014 as an executive producer for HBO's *Vice*?

Trivia Answer: Bill Maher

JUNE

On This Date: On June 11, 1770, explorer James Cook discovered the Great Barrier Reef off the coast of Australia by crashing into it!

Birthdays: Jacques Cousteau, 1910; Vince Lombardi, 1913; Gene Wilder, 1933; Joe Montana, 1956; Hugh Laurie, 1959; Dr. Mehmet Oz, 1960; Peter Dinklage, 1969; Joshua Jackson, 1978; Diana Taurasi, 1982; Shia LaBeouf, 1986; Maya Moore, 1989

Trivia: What fast food joint is known as Hungry Jack's in Australia?

Trivia Answer: Burger King

JUNE

On This Date: On June 12, 1991, the Chicago Bulls won their first NBA championship after they beat the Los Angeles Lakers. Michael Jordan was named Finals MVP for the first of six times.

Birthdays: George H.W. Bush, 1924; Vic Damone, 1928; Anne Frank, 1929; Jim Nabors, 1930; Marv Albert, 1941; Hideki Matsui, 1974; Kendra Wilkinson, 1985

Trivia: Who won five titles as an NBA player during the 1990s and 2000s before claiming his first as a head coach in 2015 with the Golden State Warriors?

Trivia Answer: Steve Kerr (His rings came with the Bulls and Spurs as a player.)

JUNE

On This Date: On June 13, 1966, the Supreme Court ruled that police must inform suspects of their rights before questioning.

Birthdays: William Butler Yeats, 1865; Red Grange, 1903; Siegfried Fischbacher, 1939; Tim Allen, 1953; Ally Sheedy, 1962; Hannah Storm, 1962; Steve-O, 1974; Kat Dennings, 1986; Ashley & Mary-Kate Olsen, 1986; Aaron Taylor-Johnson, 1990

Trivia: *Reagan's Theme*, playing off the last name of the lead characters, is the music that is heard in the opening of what police drama?

Trivia Answer: Blue Bloods

JUNE

On This Date: On June 14, 1877, the first national observance of Flag Day was held.

Birthdays: Harriet Beecher Stowe, 1811; Alois Alzheimer, 1864; Burl Ives, 1909; Che Guevara, 1928; Donald Trump, 1946; Pat Summitt, 1952; Eric Heiden, 1958; Boy George, 1961; Steffi Graf, 1969

Trivia: Are there more red or white stripes on the U.S. flag?

Trivia Answer: Reds win, 7-6.

JUNE

15

On This Date: On June 15, 1938, Cincinnati's
Johnny Vander Meer threw his second straight no-hitter,
the only pitcher in baseball history to do so.

Birthdays: Mario Cuomo, 1932; Waylon Jennings, 1937;
Xi Jinping, 1953; Jim Belushi, 1954; Wade Boggs, 1958;
Helen Hunt, 1963; Courteney Cox, 1964; Ice Cube, 1969;
Leah Remini, 1970; Neil Patrick Harris, 1973

Trivia: What is the only number that can be added to itself or
multiplied by itself with the same result?

Trivia Answer: 2 (2 x 2 = 4 or 2 + 2 = 4)

JUNE

16

On This Date: On June 16, 1963, Valentina
Tereshkova of the Soviet Union became the first female
astronaut in space.

Birthdays: Geronimo, 1829; Stan Laurel, 1890;
Roberto Duran, 1951; Phil Mickelson, 1970; Tupac Shakur, 1971

Trivia: How old was he when John Glenn became the oldest
astronaut to travel in space: 77, 82 or 87?

Trivia Answer: 77- He flew aboard the Discovery in 1998.

JUNE

On This Date: On June 17, 1972, the Watergate burglars broke into the offices of the Democratic National Committee.

Birthdays: Igor Stravinsky, 1882; Elroy "Crazylegs" Hirsch, 1923; Newt Gingrich, 1943; Barry Manilow, 1943; Joe Piscopo, 1951; Thomas Haden Church, 1960; Greg Kinnear, 1963; Will Forte, 1970; Paulina Rubio, 1971; Venus Williams, 1980; Kendrick Lamar, 1987

Trivia: The New England Patriots were accused of breaking NFL rules in a 2015 playoff game that has since become known by what controversy?

Trivia Answer: "Deflategate"

JUNE

On This Date: On June 18, 1815, the British defeated the French in the Battle of Waterloo. You might say Napoleon had a beef with Wellington and wound up in the water "loo."

Birthdays: George Mikan, 1924; Lou Brock, 1939; Roger Ebert, 1942; Paul McCartney, 1942; Bruce Smith, 1963; Blake Shelton, 1976; Antonio Gates, 1980

Trivia: Besides deep water, what additional deterrent did medieval moats offer against those invaders who wanted to storm the castle?

Trivia Answer: The moat also served as a sewer.

JUNE

On This Date: On June 19, 1910, inspired by
YMCA worker Mrs. John Dodd, the United States celebrated
the first Father's Day, three years after Mother's Day was first
celebrated.

Birthdays: Lou Gehrig, 1903; Shirley Muldowney, 1940;
Salman Rushdie, 1947; Phylicia Rashad, 1948; Kathleen Turner,
1954; Paula Abdul, 1962; Dirk Nowitzki, 1978; Zoe Saldana, 1978;
Macklemore, 1983

Trivia: Pattie Mallette is the mother of what world-famous
celebrity?

Trivia Answer: Justin Bieber

JUNE

On This Date: On June 20, 1837, 18-year-old
Alexandrina Victoria ascended to the British throne and
became Queen Victoria.

Birthdays: Olympia Dukakis, 1931; Danny Aiello, 1933;
Len Dawson, 1935; Brian Wilson, 1942; Bob Vila, 1946;
Lionel Richie, 1949; John Goodman, 1952; Nicole Kidman, 1967;
Christopher Mintz-Plasse, 1989

Trivia: The British refer to it as noughts and crosses. What do
we call it?

Trivia Answer: Tic-tac-toe

JUNE

21

On This Date: On June 21, 1964, Jim Bunning, a father of seven at the time, celebrated Father's Day by throwing a perfect game against the Mets. It was the National League's first perfect game in 84 years.

Birthdays: Chris Pratt, 1979; Prince William, 1982; Edward Snowden, 1983; Kris Allen, 1985; Lana Del Rey, 1985

Trivia: True or false? Pele was never the leading scorer in a World Cup series.

Trivia Answer: True

JUNE

22

On This Date: On June 22, 1847, Hanson Crockett Gregory, believe it or not, invented the doughnut hole!

Birthdays: John Dillinger, 1903; Kris Kristofferson, 1936; Ed Bradley, 1941; Pete Maravich, 1947; Meryl Streep, 1949; Elizabeth Warren, 1949; Cyndi Lauper, 1953; Freddie Prinze, 1954; Erin Brockovich, 1960; Clyde Drexler, 1962; Dan Brown, 1964; Kurt Warner, 1971; Carson Daly, 1973

Trivia: Wonder Bread rocked the grocery shelves with this innovation in 1930.

Trivia Answer: Sliced bread- customers thought it was the greatest thing since, well, itself!

JUNE

23

On This Date: On June 23, 2013, Nik Wallenda became the first person to high-wire walk across a Grand Canyon area gorge as he crossed the Little Colorado River outside Canyon National Park.

Birthdays: Wilma Rudolph, 1940; Clarence Thomas, 1948; Randy Jackson, 1956; Frances McDormand, 1957; Selma Blair, 1972; Zinedine Zidane, 1972; Jason Mraz, 1977; LaDainian Tomlinson, 1979

Trivia: What is the longest river in the world?

Trivia Answer: The Nile- over 4,000 miles long

JUNE

24

On This Date: On June 24, 1947, the modern era of "flying saucers" began as Kenneth Arnold reported a formation of UFOs over Mt. Rainier, WA. Previously, the only reports of flying saucers came from nudists who spilled hot tea on their laps.

Birthdays: Henry Ward Beecher, 1813; Jack Dempsey, 1895; Al Molinaro, 1919; Jeff Beck, 1944; Minka Kelly, 1980; Lionel Messi, 1987; Mo'ne Davis, 2001

Trivia: "Ronald" won an Oscar for his role as best supporting actor in *The Deer Hunter*. Who is he?

Trivia Answer: Christopher Walken

JUNE 25

On This Date: On June 25, 1876, the Battle of Little Bighorn took place, where Lt. Col. George Custer and his 7th Cavalry were knocked out by Sioux and Cheyenne Indians.

Birthdays: George Orwell, 1903; Willis Reed, 1942; Carly Simon, 1945; Phyllis George, 1949; Sonia Sotomayor, 1954; Ricky Gervais, 1961; George Michael, 1963; Dikembe Mutombo, 1966

Trivia: Albert Leffler coined what name for the new ticket agency he co-founded in 1976 in Phoenix, AZ?

Trivia Answer: Ticketmaster

JUNE 26

On This Date: On June 26, 1945, the United Nations Charter was signed by 50 nations in San Francisco.

Birthdays: Abner Doubleday, 1819; Pearl Buck, 1892; Peter Lorre, 1904; Babe Didrikson Zaharias, 1911; Chris Isaak, 1956; Greg LeMond, 1961; Shannon Sharpe, 1968; Sean Hayes, 1970; Nick Offerman, 1970; Gretchen Wilson, 1973; Derek Jeter, 1974; Michael Vick, 1980; Ariana Grande, 1993

Trivia: What country's name comes first, alphabetically speaking?

Trivia Answer: Afghanistan

JUNE

On This Date: On June 27, 1929, Bell Labs
conducted the first transmission of color television.
That was when the NBC peacock was still an egg.

Birthdays: Helen Keller, 1880; Bob "Captain Kangaroo"
Keeshan, 1927; Ross Perot, 1930; Vera Wang, 1949; J.J. Abrams,
1966; Tobey Maguire, 1975; Khloe Kardashian, 1984

Trivia: What was the colorful name of Betty White's character
on *The Golden Girls*?

Trivia Answer: Rose Nylund

JUNE

On This Date: On June 28, 1914, Archduke
Francis Ferdinand and his wife were assassinated at Sarajevo,
Bosnia, touching off the conflict that became World War I. On
this same date in 1919, the same war ended with the signing of
the Treaty of Versailles.

Birthdays: Jean-Jacques Rousseau, 1712; Mel Brooks, 1926;
Pat Morita, 1932; Gilda Radner, 1946; Kathy Bates, 1948;
John Elway, 1960; John Cusack, 1966; Elon Musk, 1971;
Kellie Pickler, 1986

Trivia: McFadden is actually his last name, but you know this
cartoon character singularly by his first name. What is it?

Trivia Answer: Casper, as in Casper the Friendly Ghost

JUNE

On This Date: On June 29, 2007, the first Apple iPhone went on sale.

Birthdays: Harmon Killebrew, 1936; Gary Busey, 1944; Richard Lewis, 1947; Nicole Scherzinger, 1978; Kawhi Leonard, 1991

Trivia: What colleges did Apple genius Steve Jobs and Microsoft's Bill Gates graduate from?

Trivia Answer: None- Both were college dropouts. Gates attended Harvard and Jobs went to Reed College in Portland, Oregon.

JUNE

On This Date: On June 30, 1859, thousands of spectators watched French acrobat Charles Blondin cross Niagara Falls on a tightrope.

Birthdays: Lena Horne, 1917; David Alan Grier, 1956; Mike Tyson, 1966; Fantasia, 1984; Michael Phelps, 1985

Trivia: Angel Falls, with a height of 3,212 feet, is the world's largest waterfall. Where is it located?

Trivia Answer: Venezuela

JULY

On This Date: On July 1, 1963, ZIP Codes were introduced in the U.S. mail.

Birthdays: Charles Laughton, 1899; Estee Lauder, 1908; Sydney Pollack, 1934; Debbie Harry, 1945; Dan Aykroyd, 1952; Princess Diana, 1961; Carl Lewis, 1961; Andre Braugher, 1962; Pamela Anderson, 1967; Missy Elliott, 1971; Liv Tyler, 1977

Trivia: In April, 1964, the U.S. Post Office assigned the zip code 20252 to what popular figure?

Trivia Answer: Smokey Bear

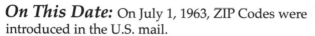

JULY

On This Date: On July 2, 1937, aviatrix Amelia Earhart disappeared over the Pacific.

Birthdays: Rene Lacoste, 1904; Thurgood Marshall, 1908; Dave Thomas, 1932; Richard Petty, 1937; Vicente Fox, 1942; Larry David, 1947; Jose Canseco, 1964; Ron Goldman, 1968; Michelle Branch, 1983; Johnny Weir, 1984; Ashley Tisdale, 1985; Lindsay Lohan, 1986; Margot Robbie, 1990

Trivia: In the banana biz, a single banana is known as a finger. Would it follow, then, that a bunch of bananas is a hand?

Trivia Answer: Yes

JULY

On This Date: On July 3, 1863, the Battle of Gettysburg in Pennsylvania ended with a major Civil War victory for the North.

Birthdays: Franz Kafka, 1883; Dave Barry, 1947; Montel Williams, 1956; Tom Cruise, 1962; Audra McDonald, 1970; Julian Assange, 1971; Olivia Munn, 1980

Trivia: When the occasion arises, the President of the United States receives a 21-gun salute. How many "guns" does the vice-president get?

Trivia Answer: 19

JULY

On This Date: On July 4, 1826, both Thomas Jefferson and John Adams died. In 1831, a third president, James Monroe, also died on Independence Day.

Birthdays: Nathaniel Hawthorne, 1804; Stephen Foster, 1826; Calvin Coolidge, 1872; Tokyo Rose, 1916; Ann Landers, 1918; Abigail Van Buren, 1918; Leona Helmsley, 1920; Neil Simon, 1927; Al Davis, 1929; George Steinbrenner, 1930; Bill Withers, 1938; Geraldo Rivera, 1943

Trivia: What's the name of the little boy on the Play-Doh can?

Trivia Answer: Play-Doh Pete

JULY

On This Date: On July 5, 1996, Dolly the sheep became the first mammal cloned from an adult cell, using the process of nuclear transfer. Dolly would live until the age of six.

Birthdays: P.T. Barnum, 1810; Katherine Helmond, 1929; Judge Joe Brown, 1947; Huey Lewis, 1950; James Lofton, 1956; Edie Falco, 1963

Trivia: What three animals move their front and hind legs on one side and then their front and hind legs on the other side when they walk?

Trivia Answer: A cat, a camel and a giraffe

JULY

On This Date: On July 6, 1933, players from the National League and the American League squared off for baseball's first All-Star Game at Comiskey Park. The AL won 4-2 as Babe Ruth belted the first homer in All-Star history.

Birthdays: John Paul Jones, 1747; Frida Kahlo, 1907; Nancy Reagan, 1921; Merv Griffin, 1925; Bill Haley, 1925; Janet Leigh, 1927; Della Reese, 1931; Dalai Lama, 1935; Ned Beatty, 1937; George W. Bush, 1946; Fred Dryer, 1946; Sylvester Stallone, 1946; Geoffrey Rush, 1951; Willie Randolph, 1954; 50 Cent, 1975; Tamera & Tia Mowry, 1978; Kevin Hart, 1979

Trivia: Name the company which, in 1877, designed the figure of a man which became the first registered trademark for a breakfast cereal.

Trivia Answer: The Quaker Oats Company

JULY

7

On This Date: On July 7, 1981, President Ronald Reagan nominated Sandra Day O'Connor to become the first female justice on the U.S. Supreme Court.

Birthdays: Satchel Paige, 1906; Doc Severinsen, 1927; Ringo Starr, 1940; Shelley Duvall, 1949; Jessica Hahn, 1959; Jim Gaffigan, 1966; Joe Sakic, 1969; Lisa Leslie, 1972; Michelle Kwan, 1980

Trivia: What was the occupation of Charlie Brown's dad?

Trivia Answer: Barber

JULY

8

On This Date: On July 8, 1776, the Liberty Bell in Philadelphia tolled, summoning citizens to the first public reading of the *Declaration of Independence*.

Birthdays: John D. Rockefeller, 1839; Nelson Rockefeller, 1908; Roone Arledge, 1931; Steve Lawrence, 1935; Jeffrey Tambor, 1944; Wolfgang Puck, 1949; Kevin Bacon, 1958; Toby Keith, 1961; Beck, 1970; Jaden Smith, 1998

Trivia: Crowning Achievement: How many spikes are atop the Statue of Liberty's head and, for extra credit, what do they represent?

Trivia Answer: 7 (They represent the seven seas and the seven continents of the world.)

JULY

On This Date: On July 9, 1877, the Wimbledon tennis tournament began. The Gentlemen's Singles tournament, won by W. Spencer Gore, was the only event at the first Wimbledon.

Birthdays: Elias Howe, 1819; Donald Rumsfeld, 1932; Brian Dennehy, 1938; Dean Koontz, 1945; O.J. Simpson, 1947; John Tesh, 1952; Tom Hanks, 1956; Courtney Love, 1964; Jack White, 1975; Fred Savage, 1976

Trivia: What does the S&P stand for in the S&P 500 stock market index?

Trivia Answer: Standard and Poor's

JULY

On This Date: On July 10, 1999, the U.S. women won the World Cup over China in thrilling fashion. After a scoreless regulation and overtime, Brandi Chastain's dramatic shootout goal gave her team a 5-4 win on penalty kicks.

Birthdays: James Whistler, 1834; David Brinkley, 1920; Fred Gwynne, 1926; Arthur Ashe, 1943; Arlo Guthrie, 1947; Andre Dawson, 1954; Sofia Vergara, 1972; Adrian Grenier, 1976; Chiwetel Ejiofor, 1977; Jessica Simpson, 1980; Antonio Brown, 1988

Trivia: What country embarrassed host Brazil, 7-1, in the 2014 World Cup semifinals, before going on to defeat Argentina to win it all?

Trivia Answer: Germany

JULY

On This Date: On July 11, 1804, Alexander Hamilton and Vice President Aaron Burr held their duel. Hamilton missed... Burr didn't.

Birthdays: John Quincy Adams, 1767; E.B. White, 1899; Yul Brynner, 1920; Giorgio Armani, 1934; Richie Sambora, 1959; Lisa Rinna, 1963; Lil' Kim, 1975; Caroline Wozniacki, 1990; Alessia Cara, 1996

Trivia: Buffalo Bill Cody gave what sharpshooter the nickname "Little Sure Shot"?

Trivia Answer: Annie Oakley

JULY

On This Date: On July 12, 1862, the Congressional Medal of Honor was created.

Birthdays: Julius Caesar, 100 BC; Henry David Thoreau, 1817; Milton Berle, 1908; Bill Cosby, 1937; Richard Simmons, 1948; Cheryl Ladd, 1951; Kristi Yamaguchi, 1971; Brock Lesnar, 1977; Malala Yousafzai, 1997

Trivia: What country pop music group is a trio composed of Hillary Scott, Charles Kelley and Dave Haywood?

Trivia Answer: Lady Antebellum

JULY 13

On This Date: On July 13, 1923, a 50-foot-tall sign spelling out "HOLLYWOODLAND" was dedicated in the Hollywood Hills. (The last four letters were removed in 1949.)

Birthdays: Johnny Gilbert, 1924; Jack Kemp, 1935; Patrick Stewart, 1940; Harrison Ford, 1942; Cheech Marin, 1946; Spud Webb, 1963; Ken Jeong, 1969

Trivia: What two 15-letter words are spelled exactly the same except for the first letter?

Trivia Answer: Nationalization and rationalization

JULY 14

On This Date: On July 14, 1790, Bastille Day was first celebrated. It came one year after citizens of Paris stormed the Bastille and freed seven prisoners during the French Revolution.

Birthdays: Woody Guthrie, 1912; Gerald Ford, 1913; John Chancellor, 1927; Vincent Pastore, 1946; Jane Lynch, 1960; Matthew Fox, 1966; Darrelle Revis, 1985; Conor McGregor, 1988

Trivia: The last original comic strip of it appeared February 13, 2000. Coincidentally, its creator died the night before. What's the name of it?

Trivia Answer: Peanuts- Charles M. Schulz, of course, was the creator.

JULY

On This Date: On July 15, 2007, the Philadelphia
Phillies became the first pro sports team in American
history to lose 10,000 games.

Birthdays: Rembrandt, 1606; Clement Moore, 1779; Alex
Karras, 1935; Linda Ronstadt, 1946; Arianna Huffington, 1950;
Jesse Ventura, 1951; John Stallworth, 1952; Barry Melrose, 1956;
Forest Whitaker, 1961; Brigitte Nielsen, 1963; Brian Austin Green,
1973; Taylor Kinney, 1981

Trivia: In what facility is tennis' U.S. Open annually held?

Trivia Answer: Arthur Ashe Stadium, in Flushing, N.Y.

JULY

On This Date: On July 16, 1941, Joe DiMaggio
extended his record consecutive game hitting streak to 56
games. The Yankee's historic streak would end the following
night against Cleveland.

Birthdays: Shoeless Joe Jackson, 1887; Orville Redenbacher,
1907; Ginger Rogers, 1911; Will Ferrell, 1967; Barry Sanders, 1968;
Corey Feldman, 1971; Carli Lloyd, 1982

Trivia: Once the tallest building in the world, the Willis Tower
in Chicago was formerly known as...?

Trivia Answer: The Sears Tower

JULY

On This Date: On July 17, 1955, Disneyland televised its grand opening in Anaheim, California, in ceremonies led by Walt Disney himself.

Birthdays: John Jacob Astor, 1763; James Cagney, 1899; Art Linkletter, 1912; Phyllis Diller, 1917; Diahann Carroll, 1935; Donald Sutherland, 1935; Camilla Parker Bowles, 1947; David Hasselhoff, 1952; Angela Merkel, 1954; Mark Burnett, 1960; Luke Bryan, 1976

Trivia: In 1995, Pixar and Walt Disney Pictures brought us the first full-length computer-generated movie ever made. What is it?

Trivia Answer: Toy Story

JULY

On This Date: On July 18, 1969, Edward Kennedy's car plunged off the Chappaquiddick Bridge, killing passenger Mary Jo Kopechne.

Birthdays: Red Skelton, 1913; Nelson Mandela, 1918; John Glenn, 1921; Dick Button, 1929; Dion DiMucci, 1939; Joe Torre, 1940; Steve Forbes, 1947; Nick Faldo, 1957; Elizabeth McGovern, 1961; Wendy Williams, 1964; Vin Diesel, 1967; Anfernee Hardaway, 1971; M.I.A., 1975; Kristen Bell, 1980; Chace Crawford, 1985

Trivia: What actor stars as politician Frank Underwood in the Netflix hit series *House of Cards*?

Trivia Answer: Kevin Spacey

JULY

On This Date: On July 19, 1980, the Summer Olympics began in Moscow. Dozens of nations, including the U.S., boycotted the Games because of Soviet military intervention in Afghanistan.

Birthdays: Lizzie Borden, 1860; George McGovern, 1922; Brian May, 1947; Stuart Scott, 1965; Benedict Cumberbatch, 1976

Trivia: At what point in the holiday season does "Cyber Monday" fall?

Trivia Answer: It is the Monday following "Black Friday", which follows Thanksgiving.

JULY

On This Date: On July 20, 1969, the lunar module from Apollo 11 touched down, and Neil Armstrong became the first human to walk on the moon.

Birthdays: Sir Edmund Hillary, 1919; Natalie Wood, 1938; Larry Craig, 1945; Carlos Santana, 1947; Chris Cornell, 1964; Sandra Oh, 1971; Omar Epps, 1973; Ray Allen, 1975; Gisele Bundchen, 1980; Stephen Strasburg, 1988; Ben Simmons, 1996

Trivia: "We Try Harder" was the former slogan of which major car rental company?

Trivia Answer: Avis

JULY

On This Date: On July 21, 1983, the lowest natural temperature ever recorded was set in Vostok, Antarctica. The thermometer plummeted to 129 degrees below zero.

Birthdays: Ernest Hemingway, 1899; Don Knotts, 1924; Janet Reno, 1938; Cat Stevens, 1948; Garry Trudeau, 1948; Robin Williams, 1951; Jon Lovitz, 1957; Brandi Chastain, 1968; Ali Landry, 1973; Josh Hartnett, 1978

Trivia: A normal body temperature is how many degrees in Centigrade?

Trivia Answer: 37 degrees

JULY

On This Date: On July 22, 1934, John Dillinger, Public Enemy #1, was gunned down by federal agents in Chicago after being betrayed by the woman in red. Dillinger had gone to the movies to see Myrna Loy in *Manhattan Melodrama*.

Birthdays: Dan Rowan, 1922; Bob Dole, 1923; Alex Trebek, 1940; Danny Glover, 1946; Albert Brooks, 1947; Don Henley, 1947; Willem Dafoe, 1955; John Leguizamo, 1964; David Spade, 1964; Tim Brown, 1966; Keyshawn Johnson, 1972; Rufus Wainwright, 1973; Selena Gomez, 1992; Prince George, 2013

Trivia: What President was the first to be born an American citizen?

Trivia Answer: Martin Van Buren

JULY

On This Date: On July 23, 1984, Vanessa Williams became the first Miss America to resign after nude photographs of her surfaced and scandalized the executives of the pageant.

Birthdays: Pee Wee Reese, 1918; Don Drysdale, 1936; Don Imus, 1940; Woody Harrelson, 1961; Slash, 1965; Gary Payton, 1968; Philip Seymour Hoffman, 1967; Alison Krauss, 1971; Marlon Wayans, 1972; Nomar Garciaparra, 1973; Monica Lewinsky, 1973; Maurice Greene, 1974; Daniel Radcliffe, 1989

Trivia: Vanessa Williams' *Colors of the Wind* won the Academy Award for Best Original Song in 1995. What movie was it from?

Trivia Answer: Pocahontas

JULY

On This Date: On July 24, 1938, instant coffee was invented. Unfortunately, it would be many years before they cracked the formula for hot water.

Birthdays: Simon Bolivar, 1783; Amelia Earhart, 1897; Gallagher, 1946; Michael Richards, 1949; Karl Malone, 1963; Barry Bonds, 1964; Kristin Chenoweth, 1968; Jennifer Lopez, 1969; Anna Paquin, 1982; Bindi Irwin, 1998

Trivia: Name the three U.S. states spelled with only four letters.

Trivia Answer: Ohio, Iowa and Utah

JULY

On This Date: On July 25, 1866, Ulysses S.
Grant was named General of the Army, the first officer
in the United States to hold that rank.

Birthdays: Walter Brennan, 1894; Estelle Getty, 1923;
Rita Marley, 1946; Walter Payton, 1954; Matt LeBlanc, 1967

Trivia: Who is the last president that didn't graduate from
college?

Trivia Answer: Harry S. Truman

JULY

On This Date: On July 26, 1947, President Harry
Truman signed the National Security Act, creating the
Department of Defense, the Central Intelligence Agency,
the National Security Council and the Joint Chiefs of Staff.

Birthdays: George Bernard Shaw, 1856; Carl Jung, 1875;
Aldous Huxley, 1894; Gracie Allen, 1895; Vivian Vance, 1909;
Stanley Kubrick, 1928; Mick Jagger, 1943; Helen Mirren, 1945;
Dorothy Hamill, 1956; Kevin Spacey, 1959; Sandra Bullock, 1964;
Jeremy Piven, 1965; Chris Harrison, 1971; Kate Beckinsale, 1973

Trivia: He was born Curtis Jackson but he got a name
"change" when he went into show business. Who is he?

Trivia Answer: 50 Cent

JULY

On This Date: On July 27, 1940, *Billboard* magazine published its first top-selling record chart.

Birthdays: Leo Durocher, 1905; Norman Lear, 1922; Jerry Van Dyke, 1931; Peggy Fleming, 1948; Bill Engvall, 1957; Triple H, 1969; Maya Rudolph, 1972; Alex Rodriguez, 1975; Jordan Spieth, 1993

Trivia: How many keys are on a piano?

Trivia Answer: 88 – 52 white and 36 black

JULY

On This Date: On July 28, 1945, a U.S. Army bomber crashed into the 79th floor of the Empire State Building in New York City, killing 14 people.

Birthdays: Beatrix Potter, 1866; Jackie Kennedy Onassis, 1929; Bill Bradley, 1943; Jim Davis, 1945; Sally Struthers, 1947; Hugo Chavez, 1954; Lori Loughlin, 1964; Dana White, 1969; Elizabeth Berkley, 1972

Trivia: What was the name of the city coffeehouse that the *Friends* gang hung out in from 1994-2004?

Trivia Answer: Central Perk

JULY

On This Date: On July 29, 1958, NASA was founded.

Birthdays: Benito Mussolini, 1883; Clara Bow, 1905; Dag Hammarskjold, 1905; Peter Jennings, 1938; Ken Burns, 1953; Tim Gunn, 1953; Martina McBride, 1966; Wil Wheaton, 1972

Trivia: Which has the most teams: the NFL, NBA, NHL or MLB?

Trivia Answer: The NFL, 32 (The others have 30.)

JULY

On This Date: On July 30, 1956, President Dwight Eisenhower declared "In God We Trust" to be the official U.S. motto.

Birthdays: Henry Ford, 1863; Casey Stengel, 1890; Bud Selig, 1934; Paul Anka, 1941; Arnold Schwarzenegger, 1947; Anita Hill, 1956; Laurence Fishburne, 1961; Lisa Kudrow, 1963; Vivica A. Fox, 1964; Terry Crews, 1968; Tom Green, 1971; Hilary Swank, 1974; Misty May-Treanor, 1977; Jaime Pressly, 1977; Hope Solo, 1981; Gina Rodriguez, 1984

Trivia: What slogan did Barack Obama use in his 2008 presidential campaign?

Trivia Answer: Change We Can Believe In

JULY

On This Date: On July 31, 1975, Teamsters Union president Jimmy Hoffa was reported missing in Detroit, Michigan. Last seen the previous afternoon in a parking lot outside a restaurant, his fate remains a mystery today, though it's believed he was murdered by organized crime figures.

Birthdays: Curt Gowdy, 1919; Mark Cuban, 1958; Wesley Snipes, 1962; J.K. Rowling, 1965; Dean Cain, 1966; Zac Brown, 1978; Evgeni Malkin, 1986; Victoria Azarenka, 1989

Trivia: If you were heading south from Detroit, what is the first foreign country you would arrive in?

Trivia Answer: Canada

AUGUST

On This Date: On August 1, 1981, MTV began broadcasting in the United States, airing its first music video, *Video Killed the Radio Star* by the Buggles.

Birthdays: Francis Scott Key, 1779; Herman Melville, 1819; Dom DeLuise, 1933; Jerry Garcia, 1942; Coolio, 1963; Edgerrin James, 1978; Madison Bumgarner, 1989

Trivia: The music video for what 2010 Justin Bieber single set a record with over six million "dislikes"?

Trivia Answer: Baby

AUGUST

On This Date: On August 2, 1776, the *Declaration of Independence* was signed.

Birthdays: Carroll O'Connor, 1924; Lamar Hunt, 1932; Peter O'Toole, 1932; Wes Craven, 1939; Lance Ito, 1950; Mary-Louise Parker, 1964; Kevin Smith, 1970; Sam Worthington, 1976

Trivia: What First Lady appeared in a special episode of *Diff'rent Strokes* to promote her "Just Say No" campaign?

Trivia Answer: Nancy Reagan

AUGUST

On This Date: On August 3, 1492, Christopher Columbus set sail from Spain on his way to the New World and the discovery of America. The voyage cost about $7,000, which included his personal salary of $300 a year.

Birthdays: Tony Bennett, 1926; Marv Levy, 1928; Martin Sheen, 1940; Martha Stewart, 1941; James Hetfield, 1963; Tom Brady, 1977; Evangeline Lilly, 1979; Ryan Lochte, 1984

Trivia: What was the full name of the Skipper on *Gilligan's Island*?

Trivia Answer: Jonas Grumby

AUGUST

On This Date: On August 4, 1693, Dom Perignon invented champagne. Now, if you could find a bottle of that vintage, you'd really have something!

Birthdays: Louis Vuitton, 1821; Elizabeth the Queen Mother, 1900; Louis Armstrong, 1901; Maurice Richard, 1921; Richard Belzer, 1944; John Riggins, 1949; Billy Bob Thornton, 1955; Barack Obama, 1961; Roger Clemens, 1962; Jeff Gordon, 1971; Meghan, Dutchess of Sussex (born Rachel Meghan Markle), 1981; Cole & Dylan Sprouse, 1992

Trivia: If you suffer from anosmia, what is it that you cannot do?

Trivia Answer: Smell

AUGUST

On This Date: On August 5, 1957, Dick Clark began hosting *American Bandstand* on ABC.

Birthdays: Joseph Merrick, 1862; Neil Armstrong, 1930; Herb Brooks, 1937; Loni Anderson, 1945; Maureen McCormick, 1956; Patrick Ewing, 1962; Adam Yauch, 1964; Lolo Jones, 1982

Trivia: What does "BMW" stand for?

Trivia Answer: Bayerische Motoren Werke (Translated it's Bavarian Motor Works.)

AUGUST

On This Date: On August 6, 1926, Gertrude Ederle became the first woman to swim across the English Channel. She reached the mark in 14 and a half hours.

Birthdays: Alfred Tennyson, 1809; Lucille Ball, 1911; Robert Mitchum, 1917; Andy Warhol, 1928; Catherine Hicks, 1951; David Robinson, 1965; M. Night Shyamalan, 1970; Geri Halliwell, 1972; Vera Farmiga, 1973; JonBenet Ramsey, 1990

Trivia: Whose 2012 hit *Call Me Maybe* hit #1 on the charts in numerous countries?

Trivia Answer: Carly Rae Jepsen

AUGUST

On This Date: On August 7, 2007, Barry Bonds hit home run #756, breaking the all-time record of Hank Aaron. Bonds would finish his career with 762 homers.

Birthdays: James Randi, 1928; Tobin Bell, 1942; Garrison Keillor, 1942; B.J. Thomas, 1942; David Duchovny, 1960; Charlize Theron, 1975; Sidney Crosby, 1987; Mike Trout, 1991

Trivia: Can you name the first U.S. president to play Little League baseball?

Trivia Answer: George W. Bush

AUGUST

On This Date: On August 8, 1992, the U.S. men's basketball team cruised to gold at the Barcelona Olympics. The "Dream Team" featured NBA players for the first time.

Birthdays: Esther Williams, 1921; Dustin Hoffman, 1937; Connie Stevens, 1938; Robin Quivers, 1952; Deborah Norville, 1958; The Edge, 1961; Scott Stapp, 1973; JC Chasez, 1976; Drew Lachey, 1976; Roger Federer, 1981

Trivia: How long is a tennis court: 68', 78' or 88'?

Trivia Answer: 78'

AUGUST

On This Date: On August 9, 1974, Gerald Ford was sworn in as the 38th president of the United States following Richard Nixon's resignation.

Birthdays: Bob Cousy, 1928; Rod Laver, 1938; Sam Elliott, 1944; Melanie Griffith, 1957; Michael Kors, 1959; Whitney Houston, 1963; Brett Hull, 1964; Hoda Kotb, 1964; Deion Sanders, 1967; Gillian Anderson, 1968; Eric Bana, 1968; Chris Cuomo, 1970; Chamique Holdsclaw, 1977; Anna Kendrick, 1985

Trivia: Can you identify the foreign capital named after the fifth U.S. president and the country where it's located?

Trivia Answer: Monrovia, Liberia

AUGUST

On This Date: On August 10, 1962, Marvel Comics superhero Spider-Man made his first appearance in issue 15 of *Amazing Fantasy*.

Birthdays: Herbert Hoover, 1874; Jimmy Dean, 1928; Eddie Fisher, 1928; Rosanna Arquette, 1959; Antonio Banderas, 1960; Justin Theroux, 1971; Angie Harmon, 1972

Trivia: On what day is Superman's birthday?

Trivia Answer: February 29

AUGUST

On This Date: On August 11, 1934, the first prisoners arrived on "The Rock", Alcatraz, San Francisco Bay.

Birthdays: Alex Haley, 1921; Mike Douglas, 1925; Carl Rowan, 1925; Jerry Falwell, 1933; Marilyn vos Savant, 1946; Steve Wozniak, 1950; Hulk Hogan, 1953; Viola Davis, 1965; Joe Rogan, 1967; Chris Hemsworth, 1983

Trivia: What organization has won the most Nobel Peace Prizes?

Trivia Answer: International Committee of the Red Cross

AUGUST

On This Date: On August 12, 1994, Major League Baseball players went on strike. The result would be the cancellation of the World Series, as baseball became the first sport in history to lose its postseason to a labor dispute.

Birthdays: Christy Mathewson, 1880; Cecil B. DeMille, 1881; George Hamilton, 1939; Pete Sampras, 1971; Casey Affleck, 1975; Plaxico Burress, 1977

Trivia: What part of the *Bible* is known as the "Decalogue"?

Trivia Answer: The Ten Commandments

AUGUST

On This Date: On August 13, 1961, the East German government closed the border between East and West Berlin. The Berlin Wall was built later that week and stood until 1989.

Birthdays: Annie Oakley, 1860; Alfred Hitchcock, 1899; Ben Hogan, 1912; Fidel Castro, 1926; Don Ho, 1930; Janet Yellen, 1946; Dan Fogelberg, 1951; Danny Bonaduce, 1959; Steve Higgins, 1963; James Morrison, 1984

Trivia: Years ago, if you chucked a "Pluto Platter", what were you doing?

Trivia Answer: Throwing a Frisbee

AUGUST

On This Date: On August 14, 2003, a blackout occurred throughout parts of the northeastern U.S. and eastern Canada. A massive power outage, it was the largest blackout in North American history, affecting 50 million people.

Birthdays: Doc Holliday, 1851; Wellington Mara, 1916; David Crosby, 1941; Steve Martin, 1945; Gary Larson, 1950; Rusty Wallace, 1956; Marcia Gay Harden, 1959; Magic Johnson, 1959; Halle Berry, 1966; Mila Kunis, 1983; Spencer Pratt, 1983; Tim Tebow, 1987

Trivia: How many New England states are there?

Trivia Answer: 6 (Connecticut, Massachusetts, Maine, New Hampshire, Rhode Island and Vermont)

AUGUST

On This Date: On August 15, 1969, the Woodstock music festival began on Max Yasgur's 600-acre dairy farm.

Birthdays: Napoleon Bonaparte, 1769; Julia Child, 1912; Mike Connors, 1925; Melinda Gates, 1964; Debra Messing, 1968; Anthony Anderson, 1970; Ben Affleck, 1972; Kerri Walsh Jennings, 1978; Carl Edwards, 1979; Joe Jonas, 1989; Jennifer Lawrence, 1990

Trivia: Who did Johnny and the Moondogs eventually become?

Trivia Answer: They went on to become the Foreverly Brothers and the Moonshiners, the Quarrymen Skiffle Group and, finally, the Beatles.

AUGUST 16

On This Date: On August 16, 1977, news came from Memphis that the King was dead, but it seems that it didn't take. Ever since, Elvis has been spotted at filling stations, 7-Elevens and Mr. Donut Shops all over the heartland.

Birthdays: Eydie Gorme, 1928; Robert Culp, 1930; Frank Gifford, 1930; Kathie Lee Gifford, 1953; James Cameron, 1954; Angela Bassett, 1958; Madonna, 1958; Timothy Hutton, 1960; Steve Carell, 1962; Vanessa Carlton, 1980

Trivia: What happens to your social security number when you die?

Trivia Answer: The numbers are retired, naturally. The nine digit combination gives them about one billion to choose from, so unless we extend benefits to the rest of the world, we have plenty of numbers left.

AUGUST 17

On This Date: On August 17, 2008, Michael Phelps won his eighth gold medal at the Beijing Summer Games, breaking Mark Spitz's record for the most golds in a single Olympics. The mark was set in the 4×100-meter medley relay.

Birthdays: Davy Crockett, 1786; Samuel Goldwyn, 1879; Mae West, 1893; Maureen O'Hara, 1920; Francis Gary Powers, 1929; Robert De Niro, 1943; Guillermo Vilas, 1952; Belinda Carlisle, 1958; Sean Penn, 1960; Jon Gruden, 1963; Donnie Wahlberg, 1969; Jim Courier, 1970; Gracie Gold, 1995

Trivia: The 11th, 12th, and 13th holes at Augusta National are traditionally called what?

Trivia Answer: Amen Corner

AUGUST

On This Date: On August 18, 1868, French astronomer Pierre Jules Cesar Janssen discovered helium.

Birthdays: Meriwether Lewis, 1774; Shelley Winters, 1920; Rosalynn Carter, 1927; Roman Polanski, 1933; Roberto Clemente, 1934; Robert Redford, 1936; Martin Mull, 1943; Elayne Boosler, 1952; Patrick Swayze, 1952; Denis Leary, 1957; Timothy Geithner, 1961; Edward Norton, 1969; Christian Slater, 1969; Malcolm-Jamal Warner, 1970; Andy Samberg, 1978

Trivia: What's the name of the top-hatted Monopoly man in the board game?

Trivia Answer: Rich Uncle Pennybags

AUGUST

On This Date: On August 19, 1977, comedian Groucho Marx, the best known of the Marx Brothers, died in Los Angeles, California.

Birthdays: Orville Wright, 1871; Coco Chanel, 1883; Malcolm Forbes, 1919; Fred Thompson, 1942; Bill Clinton, 1946; Tipper Gore, 1948; John Stamos, 1963; Kyra Sedgwick, 1965; Lee Ann Womack, 1966; Matthew Perry, 1969; Christina Perri, 1986; Romeo Miller, 1989

Trivia: You have ten seconds... The name of which famous talk show host, spelled backwards, is one of the Marx brothers?

Trivia Answer: Time's up! The answer is...Oprah.

AUGUST

On This Date: On August 20, 1882,
Tchaikovsky's *1812 Overture* premiered in Moscow.

Birthdays: Benjamin Harrison, 1833; Don King, 1931;
Ron Paul, 1935; Isaac Hayes, 1942; Connie Chung, 1946;
Robert Plant, 1948; Al Roker, 1954; Fred Durst, 1970;
Amy Adams, 1974; Andrew Garfield, 1983; Demi Lovato, 1992

Trivia: What baseball stadium began the tradition of the
"Sausage Race"?

*Trivia Answer: County Stadium in Milwaukee - The tradition continued when the
Brewers moved into Miller Park in 2001.*

AUGUST

On This Date: On August 21, 1959, the flag got
its full complement of stars as Hawaii became the last state
to join the union.

Birthdays: Jack Buck, 1924; Princess Margaret, 1930;
Wilt Chamberlain, 1936; Kenny Rogers, 1938; Kim Cattrall, 1956;
Jim McMahon, 1959; Amy Fisher, 1974; Kelis, 1979;
Usain Bolt, 1986; Hayden Panettiere, 1989; Bo Burnham, 1990

Trivia: How many letters are in the Hawaiian alphabet:
13, 23 or 33?

Trivia Answer: 13

AUGUST

On This Date: On August 22, 1851, the first international yacht race took place. The sole U.S. entry, the America, won the event that is now known as the America's Cup.

Birthdays: Ray Bradbury, 1920; Norman Schwarzkopf, 1934; Valerie Harper, 1939; Carl Yastrzemski, 1939; Bill Parcells, 1941; Steve Kroft, 1945; Cindy Williams, 1947; Diana Nyad, 1949; Paul Molitor, 1956; Tori Amos, 1963; Ty Burrell, 1967; Kristen Wiig, 1973; James Corden, 1978

Trivia: What is the real last name of father and son acting tandem Martin and Charlie Sheen?

Trivia Answer: Estevez

AUGUST

On This Date: On August 23, 1989, Victoria Brucker of San Pedro, California, became the first U.S. girl to play in the Little League World Series.

Birthdays: Gene Kelly, 1912; Shelley Long, 1949; Rick Springfield, 1949; James Van Praagh, 1958; Jay Mohr, 1970; River Phoenix, 1970; Kobe Bryant, 1978; Natalie Coughlin, 1982; Jeremy Lin, 1988

Trivia: How far is it from home plate to first base on a Little League field?

Trivia Answer: 60 feet

AUGUST

On This Date: On August 24, 1989,
Commissioner Bart Giamatti announced a permanent
banishment from baseball for Pete Rose.

Birthdays: Yasser Arafat, 1929; Vince McMahon, 1945;
Paulo Coelho, 1947; Mike Shanahan, 1952; Mike Huckabee, 1955;
Steve Guttenberg, 1958; Cal Ripken, Jr., 1960; Craig Kilborn,
1962; Marlee Matlin, 1965; Reggie Miller, 1965; Dave Chappelle,
1973; Chad Michael Murray, 1981; Rupert Grint, 1988

Trivia: On what show did Vince, E, Turtle and Johnny Drama
live the Hollywood lifestyle after growing up together in
Queens, New York?

Trivia Answer: Entourage

AUGUST

On This Date: On August 25, 1939, *The Wizard
of Oz* opened to national audiences.

Birthdays: Ivan the Terrible, 1530; George Wallace, 1919;
Althea Gibson, 1927; Sean Connery, 1930; Regis Philbin, 1931;
Gene Simmons, 1949; Elvis Costello, 1954; Tim Burton, 1958;
Billy Ray Cyrus, 1961; Albert Belle, 1966; Rachael Ray, 1968;
Claudia Schiffer, 1970; Marvin Harrison, 1972; Blake Lively, 1987

Trivia: Name the only X-rated movie to win a Best Picture
Oscar.

Trivia Answer: Midnight Cowboy, *starring Dustin Hoffman and Jon Voight*

AUGUST

On This Date: On August 26, 1920, the 19th Amendment, which guaranteed women the right to vote, was adopted into the U.S. Constitution.

Birthdays: Mother Teresa, 1910; Ben Bradlee, 1921; Irving R. Levine, 1922; Geraldine Ferraro, 1935; Branford Marsalis, 1960; Melissa McCarthy, 1970; Macaulay Culkin, 1980; Chris Pine, 1980; James Harden, 1989; KeKe Palmer, 1993

Trivia: What amendment to the U.S. Constitution abolished slavery?

Trivia Answer: The 13th Amendment

AUGUST

On This Date: On August 27, 1859, the first U.S. oil well was created accidentally by an engineer sinking a shaft in Titusville, PA. Oh well, you know what they say - oil's well that ends well.

Birthdays: Lyndon B. Johnson, 1908; Paul Reubens, 1952; Yolanda Adams, 1961; Cesar Millan, 1969; Jim Thome, 1970; Aaron Paul, 1979; Breanna Stewart, 1994

Trivia: EVOO stands for extra-virgin olive oil and became a dictionary word in 2007 thanks to what TV celebrity cook?

Trivia Answer: Rachael Ray

AUGUST

On This Date: On August 28, 1963, Dr. Martin Luther King, Jr. made his "I Have a Dream..." speech in Washington, D.C.

Birthdays: Lou Piniella, 1943; Daniel Stern, 1957; Scott Hamilton, 1958; Jennifer Coolidge, 1961; David Fincher, 1962; Shania Twain, 1965; Jack Black, 1969; Jason Priestley, 1969; LeAnn Rimes, 1982; Florence Welch, 1986

Trivia: Which NBA great has never worn the #23 during his career: Michael Jordan, Kobe Bryant or LeBron James?

Trivia Answer: Kobe Bryant

AUGUST

On This Date: On August 29, 2005, the worst natural disaster in U.S. history occurred as Hurricane Katrina slammed into the Gulf Coast, making landfall near New Orleans, Louisiana.

Birthdays: John Locke, 1632; Ingrid Bergman, 1915; Isabel Sanford, 1917; John McCain, 1936; Elliott Gould, 1938; Michael Jackson, 1958; Lea Michele, 1986

Trivia: In order to be designated a hurricane, a wind must have a minimum speed of how many miles per hour: 74, 84 or 94?

Trivia Answer: 74

AUGUST

On This Date: On August 30, 1978, Japanese
baseball legend Sadaharu Oh hit his 800th career home run.

Birthdays: Mary Shelley, 1797; Ted Williams, 1918;
Warren Buffett, 1930; Lewis Black, 1948; Cameron Diaz, 1972;
Andy Roddick, 1982

Trivia: In the 1800s, Dr. Miles' Compound Extract of Tomato
was sold as a medicine. What is it known as today?

Trivia Answer: Ketchup

AUGUST

On This Date: On August 31, 1997, England's
Princess Diana and Dodi Fayed died when their car
crashed in Paris while dodging paparazzi.

Birthdays: Fredric March, 1897; Buddy Hackett, 1924;
James Coburn, 1928; Frank Robinson, 1935; Van Morrison, 1945;
Itzhak Perlman, 1945; Tom Coughlin, 1946; Richard Gere, 1949;
Marcia Clark, 1953; Edwin Moses, 1955; Hideo Nomo, 1968;
Debbie Gibson, 1970; Chris Tucker, 1971; Larry Fitzgerald, 1983

Trivia: Of Prince Harry and Prince William of Wales, which
brother is older?

Trivia Answer: Prince William was born in 1982, Prince Harry in '84

SEPTEMBER

On This Date: On September 1, 1972, the great chess war ended as Bobby Fischer defeated Boris Spassky for the world title.

Birthdays: Rocky Marciano, 1923; Conway Twitty, 1933; Alan Dershowitz, 1938; Lily Tomlin, 1939; Barry Gibb, 1946; Dr. Phil McGraw, 1950; Gloria Estefan, 1957; Jason Taylor, 1974; Zendaya, 1996

Trivia: What do you call the dots on dice?

Trivia Answer: Pips

SEPTEMBER

On This Date: On September 2, 1969, America's first ATM began dispensing cash at Chemical Bank in New York.

Birthdays: Liliuokalani, 1838; Robert Shapiro, 1942; Terry Bradshaw, 1948; Harvey Levin, 1950; Mark Harmon, 1951; Jimmy Connors, 1952; Eric Dickerson, 1960; Keanu Reeves, 1964; Salma Hayek, 1966

Trivia: San Francisco's Charles Fey introduced what popular gambling innovation in 1899?

Trivia Answer: The first slot machine, "Liberty Bell"

SEPTEMBER

On This Date: On September 3, 1930, the first
electric train, one of Thomas Edison's last inventions,
began service between Hoboken and Montclair in New Jersey.

Birthdays: Ferdinand Porsche, 1875; Whitey Bulger, 1929;
Albert DeSalvo, 1931; Charlie Sheen, 1965; Jennie Finch, 1980;
Shaun White, 1986

Trivia: True or false? The modern lawn sprinkler was actually
invented in ancient times as a primitive steam engine.

Trivia Answer: True - It was invented by Hero, a Greek engineer, about 2000 years ago.

SEPTEMBER

On This Date: On September 4, 1972, Mark Spitz
won his seventh gold medal of the Munich Summer Games.
Before Spitz, no one had won more than five gold medals in
an Olympics. His record, of course, would later be broken by a
fellow swimmer.

Birthdays: Paul Harvey, 1918; Raymond Floyd, 1942;
Tom Watson, 1949; Dr. Drew Pinsky, 1958; Damon Wayans, 1960;
Anthony Weiner, 1964; Mike Piazza, 1968; Beyonce Knowles,
1981; Whitney Cummings, 1982

Trivia: What are the colors of each of the five rings on the
Olympic flag?

Trivia Answer: Blue, yellow, black, green and red

SEPTEMBER

On This Date: On September 5, 2006, Katie Couric became the first solo female network news anchor in American television history on the *CBS Evening News*.

Birthdays: Jesse James, 1847; Bob Newhart, 1929; Raquel Welch, 1940; Freddie Mercury, 1946; Michael Keaton, 1951; Rose McGowan, 1973

Trivia: What is the longest-running primetime network TV program?

Trivia Answer: On the air since 1968, it's 60 Minutes, still ticking away after all these years.

SEPTEMBER

On This Date: On September 6, 1995, Baltimore's Cal Ripken, Jr. played in his 2,131st consecutive Major League Baseball game, breaking Lou Gehrig's legendary record.

Birthdays: Marquis de Lafayette, 1757; John Dalton, 1766; Jane Curtin, 1947; Carly Fiorina, 1954; Jeff Foxworthy, 1958; Chris Christie, 1962; Rosie Perez, 1964; Macy Gray, 1967; Pippa Middleton, 1983

Trivia: Two days a year there are no major professional team sporting events. What are they?

Trivia Answer: The day before and the day after Major League Baseball's All-Star Game

SEPTEMBER

On This Date: On September 7, 1979, the Entertainment and Sports Programming Network made its debut. An estimated 30,000 viewers tuned in to ESPN for the first *SportsCenter* telecast.

Birthdays: Grandma Moses, 1860; Peter Lawford, 1923; Buddy Holly, 1936; Gloria Gaynor, 1949; Peggy Noonan, 1950; Eazy-E, 1963; Shannon Elizabeth, 1973; Oliver Hudson, 1976; Evan Rachel Wood, 1987; Kevin Love, 1988

Trivia: The Milton Bradley Company has been making a living from what game since the 1860s?

Trivia Answer: The Game of Life- Originally titled The Checkered Game of Life, it dates back to the Civil War.

SEPTEMBER

On This Date: On September 8, 1974, an unconditional pardon to Richard Nixon was granted by President Gerald Ford for all federal crimes that he "committed or may have committed" while president.

Birthdays: Jimmie Rodgers, 1897; Sid Caesar, 1922; Peter Sellers, 1925; Patsy Cline, 1932; Bernie Sanders, 1941; Latrell Sprewell, 1970; David Arquette, 1971; Brooke Burke, 1971; Martin Freeman, 1971; Pink, 1979; Jonathan Taylor Thomas, 1981; Wiz Khalifa, 1987

Trivia: What's the maximum amount of years that a U.S. president may be in office?

Trivia Answer: 10 – According to the 22nd Amendment to the Constitution, this maximum would be reached by a president completing two years of the term of his/her predecessor, then being elected to two full terms.

SEPTEMBER

On This Date: On September 9, 1956, Elvis Presley sprang upon a largely unsuspecting public on the *Ed Sullivan Show*.

Birthdays: Leo Tolstoy, 1828; Colonel Harland Sanders, 1890; Otis Redding, 1941; Joe Theismann, 1949; Hugh Grant, 1960; Adam Sandler, 1966; Michael Buble, 1975; Michelle Williams, 1980; Hunter Hayes, 1991

Trivia: What unique combination made up Elvis's favorite meal?

Trivia Answer: A sandwich of peanut butter and bananas grilled in butter

SEPTEMBER

On This Date: On September 10, 1846, the world was soon to be in stitches as Elias Howe received a patent on his sewing machine.

Birthdays: Arnold Palmer, 1929; Charles Kuralt, 1934; Roger Maris, 1934; Jose Feliciano, 1945; Bill O'Reilly, 1949; Joe Perry, 1950; Chris Columbus, 1958; Colin Firth, 1960; Randy Johnson, 1963; Guy Ritchie, 1968; Ryan Phillippe, 1974; Misty Copeland, 1982

Trivia: How cold would it have to be to make the Fahrenheit and Celsius scales read the same in degrees?

Trivia Answer: -40 degrees

SEPTEMBER

On This Date: On September 11, 2001, terrorists hijacked four planes, crashing two of them into the twin towers of the World Trade Center in New York City and one into the Pentagon in Washington, D.C. The fourth, also intended for the nation's capital, crashed in western Pennsylvania. Nearly 3,000 died from the attacks.

Birthdays: O. Henry, 1862; D.H. Lawrence, 1885; Paul "Bear" Bryant, 1913; Tom Landry, 1924; Lesley Visser, 1953; Kristy McNichol, 1962; Bashar al-Assad, 1965; Moby, 1965; Harry Connick, Jr., 1967; Taraji P. Henson, 1970; Ludacris, 1977

Trivia: When the tragic news broke on the morning of September 11, President Bush was not at the White House. What was he doing?

Trivia Answer: Reading a story to elementary school students in Florida

SEPTEMBER

On This Date: On September 12, 1953, JFK married Jacqueline Bouvier in Newport, Rhode Island.

Birthdays: Jesse Owens, 1913; George Jones, 1931; Linda Gray, 1940; Barry White, 1944; Ben Folds, 1966; Louis C.K., 1967; Paul Walker, 1973; Jennifer Nettles, 1974; Ruben Studdard, 1978; Yao Ming, 1980; Jennifer Hudson, 1981; Emmy Rossum, 1986; Andrew Luck, 1989

Trivia: The same year they got married, what couple starred together in the 2000 movie *Traffic*?

Trivia Answer: Catherine Zeta-Jones and Michael Douglas

SEPTEMBER 13

On This Date: On September 13, 1970, the first New York City Marathon took place, with a $1 entry fee. Fireman Gary Muhrcke was the winner.

Birthdays: Roald Dahl, 1916; Jacqueline Bisset, 1944; Michael Johnson, 1967; Tyler Perry, 1969; Stella McCartney, 1971; Fiona Apple, 1977; Ben Savage, 1980

Trivia: A major league starting pitcher must work at least how many innings to get credit for a victory?

Trivia Answer: Five

SEPTEMBER 14

On This Date: On September 14, 1814, Francis Scott Key wrote the words to the national anthem. The melody of *The Star-Spangled Banner* comes from an old English drinking song, *To Anacreon in Heaven*.

Birthdays: Clayton Moore, 1914; Robert Herjavec, 1962; Nas, 1973; Amy Winehouse, 1983

Trivia: Who shot J.R.?

Trivia Answer: Kristin Shepard

SEPTEMBER 15

On This Date: On September 15, 1978, Muhammad Ali became the first boxer to win the world heavyweight title three times when he defeated Leon Spinks.

Birthdays: James Fenimore Cooper, 1789; William Howard Taft, 1857; Agatha Christie, 1890; Tommy Lee Jones, 1946; Oliver Stone, 1946; Pete Carroll, 1951; Dan Marino, 1961; Prince Harry, 1984

Trivia: What three Chicago Cubs players were immortalized by the Franklin P. Adams poem, *Baseball's Sad Lexicon*?

Trivia Answer: Joe Tinker, Johnny Evers and Frank Chance, the famous double play combo in the early 1900s

SEPTEMBER 16

On This Date: On September 16, 1630, the little town of Shawmut, Massachusetts, decided to change its name to Boston, and it's "bean" that ever since.

Birthdays: J.C. Penney, 1875; Allen Funt, 1914; Lauren Bacall, 1924; B.B. King, 1925; Peter Falk, 1927; Elgin Baylor, 1934; Mickey Rourke, 1952; Robin Yount, 1955; David Copperfield, 1956; Richard Marx, 1963; Molly Shannon, 1964; Marc Anthony, 1968; Amy Poehler, 1971; Flo Rida, 1979; Nick Jonas, 1992

Trivia: A vacation in India means converting your traveling money to...?

Trivia Answer: Rupees

SEPTEMBER

On This Date: On September 17, 1787, the U.S. Constitution was signed in Philadelphia, which was the inspiration for making this day to be known as Citizenship Day.

Birthdays: Hank Williams, 1923; Anne Bancroft, 1931; Orlando Cepeda, 1937; Phil Jackson, 1945; John Ritter, 1948; Kyle Chandler, 1965; Doug E. Fresh, 1966; Paula Jones, 1966; Jimmie Johnson, 1975; Alexander Ovechkin, 1985

Trivia: How many people signed the Declaration of Independence: 6, 56 or 106?

Trivia Answer: 56 – John Hancock was the first to sign.

SEPTEMBER

On This Date: On September 18, 1970, rock legend Jimi Hendrix died of drug-related causes at the age of 27 in London, England.

Birthdays: Greta Garbo, 1905; Robert Blake, 1933; Scotty Bowman, 1933; Frankie Avalon, 1940; Ben Carson, 1951; Rick Pitino, 1952; Ryne Sandberg, 1959; James Gandolfini, 1961; Holly Robinson Peete, 1964; Aisha Tyler, 1970; Lance Armstrong, 1971; Jada Pinkett Smith, 1971; James Marsden, 1973; Jason Sudeikis, 1975; Ronaldo, 1976

Trivia: In a race between a cough and a sneeze, which would win?

Trivia Answer: The sneeze wins by a nose at 100 mph, while the cough encounters congestion and only manages 50.

SEPTEMBER 19

On This Date: On September 19, 1881, President James Garfield died of complications from wounds 80 days after being shot by a disgruntled assailant, Charles Guiteau, who was seeking a government job.

Birthdays: James Lipton, 1926; Adam West, 1928; Mama Cass Elliot, 1941; Joe Morgan, 1943; Joan Lunden, 1950; Mario Batali, 1960; Trisha Yearwood, 1964; Jim Abbott, 1967; Jimmy Fallon, 1974

Trivia: What was the significance of a character named Dippy Dawg in a 1932 Disney cartoon called *Mickey's Revue*?

Trivia Answer: Dippy Dawg had not yet acquired the stage name, Goofy, that would carry him through over six decades of show-biz fame and fortune.

SEPTEMBER 20

On This Date: On September 20, 1973, Billie Jean King defeated Bobby Riggs in a "Battle of the Sexes" tennis match. An estimated 90 million people worldwide tuned in as King cruised to victory in three sets.

Birthdays: Upton Sinclair, 1878; Red Auerbach, 1917; Anne Meara, 1929; Sophia Loren, 1934; Jim Taylor, 1935; George R.R. Martin, 1948; Guy Lafleur, 1951; Gary Cole, 1956; Phillip Phillips, 1990

Trivia: In May of 1973, who did Bobby Riggs defeat in the original "Battle of the Sexes"?

Trivia Answer: Margaret Court

SEPTEMBER

On This Date: On September 21, 1970, the Cleveland Browns defeated the New York Jets in the first-ever *Monday Night Football* broadcast.

Birthdays: H.G. Wells, 1866; Larry Hagman, 1931; Leonard Cohen, 1934; Stephen King, 1947; Bill Murray, 1950; Ethan Coen, 1957; Cheryl Hines, 1965; Faith Hill, 1967; Ricki Lake, 1968; Alfonso Ribeiro, 1971; Luke Wilson, 1971; Nicole Richie, 1981; Jason Derulo, 1989

Trivia: If you hear a duck quack, is it most likely a male or a female?

Trivia Answer: Female- Male ducks usually don't produce the clear, crisp "quack." They can, but it is usually a lower-pitched grunt.

SEPTEMBER

On This Date: On September 22, 1862, President Abraham Lincoln issued the preliminary Emancipation Proclamation, declaring freedom for more than three million black slaves as of January 1, 1863.

Birthdays: Tommy Lasorda, 1927; Lute Olson, 1934; David Stern, 1942; David Coverdale, 1951; Debby Boone, 1956; Andrea Bocelli, 1958; Joan Jett, 1958; Scott Baio, 1960

Trivia: What is the nickname of the flag of the Confederate States of America?

Trivia Answer: Stars and Bars

SEPTEMBER

On This Date: On September 23, 1952, Richard Nixon made his famous "Checkers" speech, in which he vowed not to return his beloved cocker spaniel which had been a gift to his daughters from some political supporters.

Birthdays: Mickey Rooney, 1920; John Coltrane, 1926; Ray Charles, 1930; Julio Iglesias, 1943; Marty Schottenheimer, 1943; Bruce Springsteen, 1949; Jason Alexander, 1959; John Harbaugh, 1962

Trivia: Who is Frank Wills and what small but crucial role did he play in recent American history?

Trivia Answer: Wills was the 24-year-old security guard who discovered the Watergate break-in, the "third-rate burglary" that eventually toppled the Nixon administration.

SEPTEMBER

On This Date: On September 24, 1968, the CBS newsmagazine staple of Sunday evenings, *60 Minutes*, made its debut- on a Tuesday!

Birthdays: John Marshall, 1755; F. Scott Fitzgerald, 1896; Jim McKay, 1921; Jim Henson, 1936; Linda McCartney, 1941; Lou Dobbs, 1945; "Mean" Joe Greene, 1946; Phil Hartman, 1948; Rafael Palmeiro, 1964; Eddie George, 1973; Ross Mathews, 1979

Trivia: What is the third hand on a clock called?

Trivia Answer: The second hand

SEPTEMBER

On This Date: On September 25, 1965,
59-year-old Satchel Paige was the starting pitcher for the
Kansas City Athletics against the Boston Red Sox. The Negro
League legend pitched three scoreless innings and gave up just
one hit.

Birthdays: William Faulkner, 1897; Red Smith, 1905;
Phil Rizzuto, 1917; Barbara Walters, 1929; Juliet Prowse, 1936;
Michael Douglas, 1944; Cheryl Tiegs, 1947; Christopher Reeve,
1952; Heather Locklear, 1961; Scottie Pippen, 1965; Will Smith,
1968; Catherine Zeta-Jones, 1969

Trivia: Christmas cards account for 65% of all card sales
during the year. What holiday is a distant second with 25%?

Trivia Answer: Valentine's Day

SEPTEMBER

On This Date: On September 26, 1969, The
Beatles 11th album, *Abbey Road*, was released. The recording
sessions were the last in which all four Beatles participated.

Birthdays: Johnny Appleseed, 1774; T.S. Eliot, 1888; George
Gershwin, 1898; Jack LaLanne, 1914; Olivia Newton-John, 1948;
Christina Milian, 1981; Serena Williams, 1981

Trivia: What is it about the Beatles' *A Day in the Life* that can
make dogs howl?

*Trivia Answer: Paul McCartney recorded a dog whistle at the end of the song. The tone is
inaudible to humans.*

SEPTEMBER

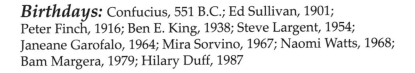

On This Date: On September 27, 1954, *The Tonight Show* made its debut with Steve Allen as the host.

Birthdays: Samuel Adams, 1722; Thomas Nast, 1840; Dick Schaap, 1934; Don Cornelius, 1936; Kathy Whitworth, 1939; Meat Loaf, 1947; Mike Schmidt, 1949; Shaun Cassidy, 1958; Steve Kerr, 1965; Gwyneth Paltrow, 1972; Lil Wayne, 1982; Avril Lavigne, 1984

Trivia: What's the only state in the U.S. that ends in "k"?

Trivia Answer: New York

SEPTEMBER

On This Date: On September 28, 1941, Ted Williams finished the season with a .406 batting average. He remains the last big leaguer to hit .400.

Birthdays: Confucius, 551 B.C.; Ed Sullivan, 1901; Peter Finch, 1916; Ben E. King, 1938; Steve Largent, 1954; Janeane Garofalo, 1964; Mira Sorvino, 1967; Naomi Watts, 1968; Bam Margera, 1979; Hilary Duff, 1987

Trivia: Can you name the last Triple Crown winner in Major League Baseball?

Trivia Answer: Miguel Cabrera, in 2012

SEPTEMBER

On This Date: On September 29, 1982, the first of seven people died after taking Extra-Strength Tylenol capsules laced with cyanide. This led to the use of safety seals on most consumer products.

Birthdays: Gene Autry, 1907; Jerry Lee Lewis, 1935; Bryant Gumbel, 1948; Andrew Dice Clay, 1957; Russell Peters, 1970; Zachary Levi, 1980; Calvin Johnson, 1985; Kevin Durant, 1988

Trivia: With help from a Facebook campaign, who became the oldest person to host *Saturday Night Live* in 2010 at the age of 88?

Trivia Answer: Betty White

SEPTEMBER

On This Date: On September 30, 1955, 24-year-old movie star James Dean died in a car crash on a California highway.

Birthdays: Buddy Rich, 1917; Truman Capote, 1924; Angie Dickinson, 1931; Johnny Mathis, 1935; Marilyn McCoo, 1943; Deborah Allen, 1953; Barry Williams, 1954; Fran Drescher, 1957; Jenna Elfman, 1971; Marion Cotillard, 1975; Martina Hingis, 1980; Dominique Moceanu, 1981

Trivia: Oklahoma's lone pro team of the four major North American sports has what weather-related moniker?

Trivia Answer: Thunder, of the NBA (Oklahoma City)

OCTOBER

On This Date: On October 1, 1962, the king of
late-night talk shows, Johnny Carson took over from Jack
Paar as host of *The Tonight Show.*

Birthdays: Walter Matthau, 1920; Jimmy Carter, 1924;
Tom Bosley, 1927; Julie Andrews, 1935; Rod Carew, 1945;
Stephen Collins, 1947; Randy Quaid, 1950; Mark McGwire, 1963;
Zach Galifianakis, 1969; Brie Larson, 1989

Trivia: When Sir Henry Royce died in 1933, the manufacturers
of the Rolls-Royce changed the monogram from red to what
color?

Trivia Answer: Black

OCTOBER

On This Date: On October 2, 1959, Rod Serling
first beckoned Americans into the *Twilight Zone.*

Birthdays: Nat Turner, 1800; Mahatma Gandhi, 1869;
Groucho Marx, 1890; Johnnie Cochran, 1937; Don McLean, 1945;
Donna Karan, 1948; Sting, 1951; Kelly Ripa, 1970

Trivia: What two Muppets share their names with characters
in *It's A Wonderful Life?*

Trivia Answer: Bert and Ernie

OCTOBER

On This Date: On October 3, 1955, Annette slapped on her first pair of giant ears as *The Mickey Mouse Club* hit the airwaves.

Birthdays: Chubby Checker, 1941; Roy Horn, 1944; Dave Winfield, 1951; Dennis Eckersley, 1954; Al Sharpton, 1954; Stevie Ray Vaughan, 1954; Fred Couples, 1959; Tommy Lee, 1962; Clive Owen, 1964; Gwen Stefani, 1969; Neve Campbell, 1973; Seann William Scott, 1976; Ashlee Simpson, 1984

Trivia: Who has been around longer: Popeye or Daffy Duck?

Trivia Answer: Popeye – He hit the deck in 1929 while Daffy didn't get down until 1937.

OCTOBER

On This Date: On October 4, 1965, Pope Paul VI made the first papal visit to the United States, during which time he celebrated a Mass at Yankee Stadium.

Birthdays: Rutherford B. Hayes, 1822; Charlton Heston, 1923; Jackie Collins, 1937; Tony La Russa, 1944; Chuck Hagel, 1946; Susan Sarandon, 1946; Russell Simmons, 1957; Liev Schreiber, 1967; Alicia Silverstone, 1976; Derrick Rose, 1988; Dakota Johnson, 1989

Trivia: Rick Swenson is a legend among those who run this Alaskan race. What is it?

Trivia Answer: The Iditarod dog sled race

OCTOBER

On This Date: On October 5, 2001, Barry Bonds passed Mark McGwire's mark with his 71st home run of the season.

Birthdays: Chester A. Arthur, 1829; Ray Kroc, 1902; Barry Switzer, 1937; Steve Miller, 1943; Bernie Mac, 1957; Neil deGrasse Tyson, 1958; Michael Andretti, 1962; Mario Lemieux, 1965; Patrick Roy, 1965; Grant Hill, 1972; Kate Winslet, 1975; Jesse Eisenberg, 1983

Trivia: "NASCAR" is the "National Association" for what?

Trivia Answer: Stock Car Auto Racing

OCTOBER

On This Date: On October 6, 1979, Pope John Paul II became the first pontiff to visit the White House.

Birthdays: George Westinghouse, 1846; Janet Gaynor, 1906; Tony Dungy, 1955; Rebecca Lobo, 1973

Trivia: In 1967, his daughter Lynda became the only child of a president to get married at the White House. Who was that president?

Trivia Answer: Lyndon B. Johnson

OCTOBER

On This Date: On October 7, 1916, Georgia Tech destroyed Cumberland, 222-0, in the most lopsided contest in the history of college football.

Birthdays: Niels Bohr, 1885; Desmond Tutu, 1931; Joy Behar, 1942; John Mellencamp, 1951; Vladimir Putin, 1952; Yo-Yo Ma, 1955; Simon Cowell, 1959; Toni Braxton, 1967; Taylor Hicks, 1976; Charles Woodson, 1976

Trivia: What is the plural of the word "moose"?

Trivia Answer: Moose

OCTOBER

On This Date: On October 8, 1871, Mrs. O'Leary's cow turned the tables on would-be barbecuers as it began the Great Chicago Fire that virtually destroyed the city.

Birthdays: Paul Hogan, 1939; Jesse Jackson, 1941; Chevy Chase, 1943; R.L. Stine, 1943; Dennis Kucinich, 1946; Sigourney Weaver, 1949; Darrell Hammond, 1955; Matt Damon, 1970; Nick Cannon, 1980; Bruno Mars, 1985; Trent Harmon, 1990; Angus T. Jones, 1993

Trivia: Standing over eight feet tall, he made his first appearance in 1969. He now has a star on the Hollywood Walk of Fame. He is…?

Trivia Answer: Big Bird

OCTOBER

On This Date: On October 9, 1888, the Washington Monument opened.

Birthdays: John Lennon, 1940; Jackson Browne, 1948; Sharon Osbourne, 1952; Tony Shalhoub, 1953; John O'Hurley, 1954; Mike Singletary, 1958; David Cameron, 1966; Steve McQueen, 1969; Annika Sorenstam, 1970; Scotty McCreery, 1993

Trivia: Which is taller: St. Louis' Gateway Arch or the Washington Monument in Washington, D.C.?

Trivia Answer: The Gateway Arch, at 630 feet, is 75 feet taller than the Washington Monument.

OCTOBER

On This Date: On October 10, 1886, Griswold Lorillard showed up at the Autumn Ball at the Tuxedo Park Country Club, New York, positively resplendent, decked out in the first formal dinner jacket. He was the talk of the town and the name "tuxedo" stuck.

Birthdays: Helen Hayes, 1900; Ben Vereen, 1946; Nora Roberts, 1950; David Lee Roth, 1954; Brett Favre, 1969; Mario Lopez, 1973; Dale Earnhardt Jr., 1974; Mya, 1979; Andrew McCutchen, 1986

Trivia: Where would you find a pintle?

Trivia Answer: Look at the nearest door- It's the pin that holds the hinge together.

OCTOBER

On This Date: On October 11, 1968, Apollo 7, the first manned Apollo mission, was launched with astronauts Wally Schirra, Donn F. Eisele and R. Walter Cunningham aboard.

Birthdays: Eleanor Roosevelt, 1884; Daryl Hall, 1946; Steve Young, 1961; Joan Cusack, 1962; Luke Perry, 1966; Jane Krakowski, 1968; Michelle Trachtenberg, 1985; Michelle Wie, 1989; Cardi B, 1992

Trivia: What does NASA stand for?

Trivia Answer: The National Aeronautics and Space Administration

OCTOBER

On This Date: On October 12, 1492, Colum… awww, you know the rest.

Birthdays: Dick Gregory, 1932; Luciano Pavarotti, 1935; Susan Anton, 1950; Hugh Jackman, 1968; Kirk Cameron, 1970; Marion Jones, 1975; Bode Miller, 1977; Josh Hutcherson, 1992

Trivia: When he started the American Messenger Company in 1907 in Seattle, Jim Casey was 19 years old. By the end of World War I, his tiny messenger service had grown considerably and he changed its name to what current outfit?

Trivia Answer: United Parcel Service

OCTOBER

On This Date: On October 13, 1792, the cornerstone of the White House was laid.

Birthdays: Margaret Thatcher, 1925; Paul Simon, 1941; Jerry Jones, 1942; Sammy Hagar, 1947; Marie Osmond, 1959; Doc Rivers, 1961; Jerry Rice, 1962; Nancy Kerrigan, 1969; Sacha Baron Cohen, 1971; Summer Sanders, 1972; Paul Pierce, 1977; Ashanti, 1980; Ian Thorpe, 1982

Trivia: What was Chuck Berry's only number one hit?

Trivia Answer: My Ding-a-Ling, 1972

OCTOBER

On This Date: On October 14, 1947, U.S. Air Force Captain Chuck Yeager became the first person to fly faster than the speed of sound.

Birthdays: William Penn, 1644; Dwight D. Eisenhower, 1890; E.E. Cummings, 1894; John Wooden, 1910; Ralph Lauren, 1939; Usher, 1978; Jared Goff, 1994

Trivia: Which grow faster, your fingernails or your toenails?

Trivia Answer: Thumbs up for your fingernails. They grow about four times faster than your toenails.

OCTOBER

On This Date: On October 15, 1917, France executed one Margaretha Zelle for her activities on behalf of Germany. History knows her as Mata Hari.

Birthdays: Friedrich Nietzsche, 1844; P.G. Wodehouse, 1881; Mario Puzo, 1920; Lee Iacocca, 1924; Penny Marshall, 1943; Jim Palmer, 1945; Tito Jackson, 1953; Emeril Lagasse, 1959

Trivia: This college basketball sportscaster is known for catchphrases like "diaper dandy" (for a freshman player) and "It's awesome baby."

Trivia Answer: Dick Vitale

OCTOBER

On This Date: On October 16, 1793, Marie "Let them eat cake" Antoinette was beheaded.

Birthdays: Noah Webster, 1758; Oscar Wilde, 1854; David Ben-Gurion, 1886; Eugene O'Neill, 1888; Angela Lansbury, 1925; Tim McCarver, 1941; Suzanne Somers, 1946; Tim Robbins, 1958; Flea, 1962; John Mayer, 1977; Bryce Harper, 1992

Trivia: Robyn Fenty, who has sold millions of albums worldwide, is known simply by her middle name. What is it?

Trivia Answer: Rihanna

OCTOBER

On This Date: On October 17, 1989, the World Series was delayed by an earthquake measuring 7.1 on the Richter scale as it rocked Candlestick Park and the San Francisco Bay area.

Birthdays: Pope John Paul I, 1912; Arthur Miller, 1915; Evel Knievel, 1938; George Wendt, 1948; Alan Jackson, 1958; Norm Macdonald, 1963; Ernie Els, 1969; Wyclef Jean, 1969; Eminem, 1972; Holly Holm, 1981; Felicity Jones, 1983

Trivia: What Christmas landmark can be found at 3159 West 11th Street in Cleveland, Ohio?

Trivia Answer: It's the house from the film A Christmas Story.

OCTOBER

On This Date: On October 18, 1867, "Seward's Folly" was consummated as the United States took possession of Alaska from the Russians.

Birthdays: Pierre Trudeau, 1919; Jesse Helms, 1921; Chuck Berry, 1926; Keith Jackson, 1928; Peter Boyle, 1935; Mike Ditka, 1939; Lee Harvey Oswald, 1939; Martina Navratilova, 1956; Thomas "Hitman" Hearns, 1958; Jean-Claude Van Damme, 1960; Wynton Marsalis, 1961; Ne-Yo, 1979; Freida Pinto, 1984; Lindsey Vonn, 1984; Zac Efron, 1987; Brittney Griner, 1990; Bristol Palin, 1990

Trivia: What Facebook creator was named *Time* magazine's Person of the Year for 2010?

Trivia Answer: Mark Zuckerberg

OCTOBER

On This Date: On October 19, 1781, Cornwallis surrendered to Washington at Yorktown, effectively ending the Revolutionary War.

Birthdays: Robert Reed, 1932; John Lithgow, 1945; Evander Holyfield, 1962; Ty Pennington, 1964; Jon Favreau, 1966; Amy Carter, 1967; John Edward, 1969; Trey Parker, 1969; Chris Kattan, 1970; Jason Reitman, 1977

Trivia: Lefty's first major championship victory came at the 2004 Masters. Who is he?

Trivia Answer: Phil Mickelson

OCTOBER

On This Date: On October 20, 2004, the Red Sox won the pennant with a 10-3 victory over the Yankees. Boston became the first team in Major League Baseball history to recover from a 3-0 postseason series deficit.

Birthdays: Dr. Joyce Brothers, 1927; Mickey Mantle, 1931; Juan Marichal, 1937; Tom Petty, 1950; Danny Boyle, 1956; Snoop Dogg, 1971; John Krasinski, 1979

Trivia: What psychological exam is commonly known as the Inkblot Test?

Trivia Answer: The Rorschach Test

OCTOBER

On This Date: On October 21, 1879, Thomas Edison's brightest idea came to light as he invented the first practical incandescent electric light bulb.

Birthdays: Alfred Nobel, 1833; Dizzy Gillespie, 1917; Whitey Ford, 1928; Judge Judy Sheindlin, 1942; Bill Russell, 1948; Benjamin Netanyahu, 1949; Carrie Fisher, 1956; Kim Kardashian, 1980

Trivia: What is the Greek equivalent to the letter D?

Trivia Answer: Delta

OCTOBER

On This Date: On October 22, 1938, the first Xerox copy was made, by American inventor Chester F. Carlson.

Birthdays: Franz Liszt, 1811; Jimmie Foxx, 1907; Christopher Lloyd, 1938; Annette Funicello, 1942; Jeff Goldblum, 1952; Bob Odenkirk, 1962; Brian Boitano, 1963; Carlos Mencia, 1967; Ichiro Suzuki, 1973; Jesse Tyler Ferguson, 1975

Trivia: Leonard Slye and Frances Octavia Smith were the real names of what famous TV western married couple of the 1950s?

Trivia Answer: Roy Rogers and Dale Evans

OCTOBER

On This Date: On October 23, 1962, 12-year-old Stevie Wonder made his first recording, *Thank You for Loving Me All the Way,* for Motown.

Birthdays: Adlai Stevenson, 1835; Johnny Carson, 1925; Pelé, 1940; Michael Crichton, 1942; Nancy Grace, 1959; Weird Al Yankovic, 1959; Doug Flutie, 1962; Ryan Reynolds, 1976; Miguel, 1985

Trivia: Would a decennial anniversary occur before or after a quindecennial anniversary?

Trivia Answer: Before- A decennial marks the 10th anniversary, a quindecennial, the 15th.

OCTOBER

On This Date: On October 24, 1826, the patent was issued for an invention that never set the world on fire, the safety match.

Birthdays: Y.A. Tittle, 1926; Kevin Kline, 1947; Monica, 1980; Tila Tequila, 1981; Drake, 1986

Trivia: In 2016, Joey Chestnut set the world record for eating how many hot dogs in 10 minutes: 50, 60, or 70?

Trivia Answer: 70

OCTOBER

On This Date: On October 25, 1972, the first
female FBI agents completed their training in Quantico, Virginia.

Birthdays: Pablo Picasso, 1881; Jack Kent Cooke, 1912;
Minnie Pearl, 1912; Marion Ross, 1928; Bob Knight, 1940;
Helen Reddy, 1941; Pedro Martinez, 1971; Craig Robinson, 1971;
Katy Perry, 1984; Ciara, 1985

Trivia: On the 100th anniversary of his death, what famous
person's autobiography was finally released in 2010?

Trivia Answer: Mark Twain

OCTOBER

On This Date: On October 26, 1881, the Earp
brothers and Doc Holliday defeated the Clanton gang at
the O.K. Corral in Tombstone, Arizona.

Birthdays: Pat Sajak, 1946; Hillary Clinton, 1947;
Jaclyn Smith, 1945; Rita Wilson, 1956; Dylan McDermott, 1961;
Keith Urban, 1967; Seth MacFarlane, 1973; Jon Heder, 1977;
Emilia Clarke, 1986

Trivia: Sergey Brin and Larry Page are the co-founders of what
Internet company?

Trivia Answer: Google

OCTOBER

On This Date: On October 27, 1994, the U.S.
prison population exceeded one million for the first time
in the nation's history.

Birthdays: Theodore Roosevelt, 1858; Dylan Thomas, 1914;
Nanette Fabray, 1920; Ralph Kiner, 1922; Sylvia Plath, 1932;
John Cleese, 1939; John Gotti, 1940; Scott Weiland, 1967;
Kelly Osbourne, 1984

Trivia: World Peace Day is observed annually on what date?

Trivia Answer: September 21

OCTOBER

On This Date: On October 28, 1886, the Statue
of Liberty was dedicated on Bedloe's Island. The inscription
"Give me your tired, your poor, your huddled masses..."
was written by Emma Lazarus.

Birthdays: Jonas Salk, 1914; Lenny Wilkens, 1937; Caitlyn
(Bruce) Jenner, 1949; Bill Gates, 1955; Mahmoud Ahmadinejad,
1956; Julia Roberts, 1967; Ben Harper, 1969; Terrell Davis, 1972;
Brad Paisley, 1972; Joaquin Phoenix, 1974; Frank Ocean, 1987

Trivia: What kind of footwear does the Statue of Liberty have
on?

Trivia Answer: Sandals

OCTOBER

On This Date: On October 29, 1929, the Great
Depression began as the stock market collapsed, causing
economic chaos which lasted until WWII.

Birthdays: Bob Ross, 1942; Richard Dreyfuss, 1947;
Kate Jackson, 1948; Drew Rosenhaus, 1966; Winona Ryder, 1971;
Gabrielle Union, 1972; Amanda Beard, 1981

Trivia: The Antoinette Perry Awards for Excellence in Theatre
is commonly referred to by what name?

Trivia Answer: Tony Awards

OCTOBER

On This Date: On October 30, 1938, Orson Welles
and the Mercury Players scared the pants off America with
their Halloween Eve broadcast of *The War of the Worlds*, in
which they presented a series of news bulletins reporting that
the Martians were invading New Jersey.

Birthdays: John Adams, 1735; Martha Jefferson, 1748;
Dick Vermeil, 1936; Grace Slick, 1939; Henry Winkler, 1945;
Andrea Mitchell, 1946; Harry Hamlin, 1951; Kevin Pollak, 1957;
Diego Maradona, 1960; Larry Wilmore, 1961; Gavin Rossdale,
1965; Matthew Morrison, 1978; Ivanka Trump, 1981; Nastia
Liukin, 1989

Trivia: The "Daily diary of the American dream" is the slogan
of what newspaper?

Trivia Answer: Wall Street Journal

OCTOBER

On This Date: On October 31, 1926, Harry Houdini made his final disappearing act on Halloween. The illusionist died at the age of 52.

Birthdays: John Keats, 1795; Juliette Low, 1860; Chiang Kai-Shek, 1887; Dale Evans, 1912; Michael Collins, 1930; Dan Rather, 1931; Michael Landon, 1936; John Candy, 1950; Jane Pauley, 1950; Nick Saban, 1951; Peter Jackson, 1961; Dermot Mulroney, 1963; Rob Schneider, 1963; Vanilla Ice, 1967; Willow Smith, 2000

Trivia: Brooklyn homemaker Jean Nidetch founded this "pound-perceptive" company in 1963.

Trivia Answer: Weight Watchers

NOVEMBER

On This Date: On November 1, 1939, Rudolph the Red-Nosed Reindeer first appeared in a pamphlet given away as a holiday promotion at a Chicago store.

Birthdays: Grantland Rice, 1880; Al Arbour, 1932; Gary Player, 1935; Larry Flynt, 1942; David Foster, 1949; Lyle Lovett, 1957; Tim Cook, 1960; Fernando Valenzuela, 1960; Anthony Kiedis, 1962; Toni Collette, 1972; Jenny McCarthy, 1972

Trivia: Designer Gloria Vanderbilt is the mother of what CNN news anchor?

Trivia Answer: Anderson Cooper

NOVEMBER

On This Date: On November 2, 1948, Harry
Truman confounded pundits and embarrassed newspaper
headline writers by defeating Dewey in the presidential election.

Birthdays: Daniel Boone, 1734; Marie Antoinette, 1755;
James K. Polk, 1795; Warren G. Harding, 1865; Burt Lancaster,
1913; k.d. lang, 1961; David Schwimmer, 1966; Scott Walker, 1967;
Nelly, 1974

Trivia: True or false? Election Day falls on the first Tuesday of
November.

Trivia Answer: False – It occurs on the first Tuesday after the first Monday of November.

NOVEMBER

On This Date: On November 3, 1952, Clarence
Birdseye, the founder of the frozen food industry, marketed
the first frozen peas.

Birthdays: Bob Feller, 1918; Charles Bronson, 1921;
Michael Dukakis, 1933; Roseanne Barr, 1952; Dennis Miller, 1953;
Phil Simms, 1955; Dolph Lundgren, 1957; Colin Kaepernick,
1987; Elizabeth Smart, 1987

Trivia: What vegetable do you discard the outside, cook the
inside, eat the outside and chuck the inside?

Trivia Answer: Corn on the cob

NOVEMBER

On This Date: On November 4, 2008, Barack
Obama was elected the 44th president of the United States
and the nation's first black chief executive.

Birthdays: Will Rogers, 1879; Walter Cronkite, 1916;
Art Carney, 1918; Doris Roberts, 1925; Laura Bush, 1946;
Kathy Griffin, 1960; Ralph Macchio, 1961; Jeff Probst, 1961;
Sean "Puffy" Combs, 1969; Matthew McConaughey, 1969;
Bethenny Frankel, 1970; Devin Hester, 1982; Dez Bryant, 1988

Trivia: Jackie Robinson was the first African-American big
league baseball player. Who was the second?

Trivia Answer: Larry Doby

NOVEMBER

On This Date: On November 5, 1781, the first
President of the United States was elected. It was not George
Washington, but John Hanson of Maryland. His official title
was "President of the United States in Congress Assembled".
He served for a year and had several successors before
Washington took over.

Birthdays: Roy Rogers, 1911; Vivien Leigh, 1913; Ike Turner,
1931; Art Garfunkel, 1941; Bill Walton, 1952; Kris Jenner, 1955;
Bryan Adams, 1959; Tilda Swinton, 1960; Tatum O'Neal, 1963;
Kevin Jonas, 1987; Odell Beckham, Jr., 1992

Trivia: What is Cap'n Crunch's first name?

Trivia Answer: Horatio

NOVEMBER

On This Date: On November 6, 1947, *Meet the Press*, the longest-running program in television history, debuted on a local Washington, D.C., station.

Birthdays: John Philip Sousa, 1854; James Naismith, 1861; Walter Johnson, 1887; Sally Field, 1946; Glenn Frey, 1948; Maria Shriver, 1955; Ethan Hawke, 1970; Rebecca Romijn, 1972; Pat Tillman, 1976; Taryn Manning, 1978; Lamar Odom, 1979; Emma Stone, 1988; Aaron Hernandez, 1989

Trivia: What soap, broadcast from 1952 to 2009, is listed in *Guinness World Records* as the longest-running TV drama in history?

Trivia Answer: Guiding Light

NOVEMBER

On This Date: On November 7, 1874, the G.O.P.'s elephant made its debut as Thomas Nast first used the pachyderm to symbolize the Republicans in a satirical cartoon for *Harper's Weekly*.

Birthdays: Marie Curie, 1867; Leon Trotsky, 1879; Albert Camus, 1913; Billy Graham, 1918; Joan Sutherland, 1926; Joni Mitchell, 1943; David Petraeus, 1952; Christopher Knight, 1957; Morgan Spurlock, 1970; Lorde, 1996

Trivia: What would you find a cruciverbalist doing in his easy chair?

Trivia Answer: A crossword puzzle

NOVEMBER

On This Date: On November 8, 1960,
Massachusetts Senator John F. Kennedy narrowly
defeated Vice President Richard M. Nixon for the
presidency of the United States.

Birthdays: Milton Bradley, 1836; Margaret Mitchell, 1900;
Bobby Bowden, 1929; Morley Safer, 1931; Bonnie Raitt, 1949;
Alfre Woodard, 1952; Leif Garrett, 1961; Gordon Ramsay, 1966;
Tara Reid, 1975; Jack Osbourne, 1985; Giancarlo Stanton, 1989

Trivia: What baseball player hit a home run for his 3,000th
career hit in 2011?

Trivia Answer: Derek Jeter

NOVEMBER

On This Date: On November 9, 1989, the first
crack in the Berlin Wall appeared as East Germany opened
many of the checkpoints in the barrier and, after 28 years,
allowed its citizens to come and go.

Birthdays: Hedy Lamarr, 1914; Spiro Agnew, 1919;
Carl Sagan, 1934; Bob Gibson, 1935; Mary Travers, 1936;
Lou Ferrigno, 1951; Chris Jericho, 1970; Nick Lachey, 1973;
Sisqó, 1978

Trivia: Willis Carrier was called the "Father of Cool" for what
comforting invention?

Trivia Answer: Air conditioning

NOVEMBER

On This Date: On November 10, 1982, the Vietnam Veterans Memorial opened in Washington, D.C.

Birthdays: Martin Luther, 1483; Richard Burton, 1925; Roy Scheider, 1932; Sinbad, 1956; Mackenzie Phillips, 1959; Tracy Morgan, 1968; Brittany Murphy, 1977; Miranda Lambert, 1983

Trivia: The liripoops come out in June and are commonly seen at what special occasion?

Trivia Answer: Graduations- They're the tail or tassel on the graduate's hat.

NOVEMBER

On This Date: On November 11, 1919, President Woodrow Wilson declared it Armistice Day, a salute to veterans who served in the U.S. Armed Forces. The national holiday was renamed Veterans Day in 1954.

Birthdays: Abigail Adams, 1744; George S. Patton, 1885; Kurt Vonnegut, 1922; Jonathan Winters, 1925; Marc Summers, 1951; Stanley Tucci, 1960; Demi Moore, 1962; Calista Flockhart, 1964; Leonardo DiCaprio, 1974

Trivia: Who starred in the comedic golf flick *Happy Gilmore*?

Trivia Answer: Adam Sandler

NOVEMBER 12

On This Date: On November 12, 1946, we celebrated the opening of America's first drive-up bank, in Chicago.

Birthdays: Elizabeth Cady Stanton, 1815; Grace Kelly, 1929; Charles Manson, 1934; Al Michaels, 1944; Neil Young, 1945; Megan Mullally, 1958; Nadia Comaneci, 1961; Sammy Sosa, 1968; Tonya Harding, 1970; Ryan Gosling, 1980; Anne Hathaway, 1982; Jason Day, 1987; Russell Westbrook, 1988

Trivia: What venue opened its comedy theatre doors in 1959 at 1616 North Wells Street in Chicago?

Trivia Answer: The Second City

NOVEMBER 13

On This Date: On November 13, 1927, the first underwater tunnel in the U.S. - the Holland Tunnel - running under the Hudson River between New York City and Jersey City, New Jersey, opened to traffic.

Birthdays: Robert Louis Stevenson, 1850; Garry Marshall, 1934; Joe Mantegna, 1947; Whoopi Goldberg, 1955; Jimmy Kimmel, 1967; Gerard Butler, 1969; Metta World Peace, 1979

Trivia: Where would you find the statements "As I see it, yes", "My reply is no" and "Better not tell you now"?

Trivia Answer: Inside a Magic 8-Ball

NOVEMBER

On This Date: On November 14, 1851, Herman Melville published *Moby-Dick*.

Birthdays: Robert Fulton, 1765; Claude Monet, 1840; Sherwood Schwartz, 1916; McLean Stevenson, 1927; Prince Charles, 1948; Condoleezza Rice, 1954; Yanni, 1954; Patrick Warburton, 1964; Curt Schilling, 1966; Josh Duhamel, 1972

Trivia: If you look at the copyright page at the front of this book, you'll see an ISBN number. What does ISBN stand for?

Trivia Answer: International Standard Book Number

NOVEMBER

On This Date: On November 15, 1926, NBC launched its broadcasting business with a radio network of 24 stations.

Birthdays: Georgia O'Keeffe, 1887; Judge Joseph Wapner, 1919; Ed Asner, 1929; Petula Clark, 1932; Sam Waterston, 1940; Beverly D'Angelo, 1951; Kevin Eubanks, 1957; Chad Kroeger, 1974; Karl-Anthony Towns, 1995

Trivia: What is friggatriskaidekaphobia?

Trivia Answer: The fear of Friday the 13th

NOVEMBER

On This Date: On November 16, 1907, Oklahoma entered the Union. Exactly 50 years later, college football's longest winning streak came to an end when the Oklahoma Sooners lost after 47 straight victories.

Birthdays: Burgess Meredith, 1907; Dwight Gooden, 1964; Lisa Bonet, 1967; Oksana Baiul, 1977; Maggie Gyllenhaal, 1977; Pete Davidson, 1993

Trivia: True or false? *Oklahoma* is the official state song of Oklahoma.

Trivia Answer: True

NOVEMBER

On This Date: On November 17, 2005, *Il Canto degli Italiani (The Song of the Italians)* officially became the Italian national anthem, some 60 years after the country became a republic.

Birthdays: Rock Hudson, 1925; Gordon Lightfoot, 1938; Martin Scorsese, 1942; Lauren Hutton, 1943; Jim Boeheim, 1944; Danny DeVito, 1944; Lorne Michaels, 1944; Tom Seaver, 1944; Howard Dean, 1948; John Boehner, 1949; RuPaul, 1960; Susan Rice, 1964; Jeff Buckley, 1966; Daisy Fuentes, 1966; Rachel McAdams, 1978; Ryan Braun, 1983

Trivia: What number means bad luck in Italy?

Trivia Answer: 17

NOVEMBER

On This Date: On November 18, 1865, Mark
Twain's first piece of fiction was published in the *New York Saturday Press*. It was called *The Celebrated Jumping Frog of Calaveras County*.

Birthdays: George Gallup, 1901; Johnny Mercer, 1909;
Alan Shepard, 1923; Susan Sullivan, 1942; Kevin Nealon, 1953;
Warren Moon, 1956; Elizabeth Perkins, 1960; Owen Wilson, 1968;
Megyn Kelly, 1970; Chloë Sevigny, 1974; David Ortiz, 1975

Trivia: What are the two ingredients that make up a nickel?

Trivia Answer: Nickel and copper

NOVEMBER

On This Date: On November 19, 1863, Abraham
Lincoln delivered one of the most famous speeches in
American history, the *Gettysburg Address*.

Birthdays: James Garfield, 1831; Tommy Dorsey, 1905;
Roy Campanella, 1921; Larry King, 1933; Dick Cavett, 1936;
Ted Turner, 1938; Calvin Klein, 1942; Ahmad Rashad, 1949;
Ann Curry, 1956; Allison Janney, 1959; Meg Ryan, 1961;
Jodie Foster, 1962; Gail Devers, 1966; Jack Dorsey, 1976;
Kerri Strug, 1977; Ryan Howard, 1979; Patrick Kane, 1988

Trivia: Stephenie Meyer is the author of what famous fantasy
romance series?

Trivia Answer: Twilight

NOVEMBER

On This Date: On November 20, 1888, William Bundy invented the first time clock, and a lot of people have wanted to punch him out ever since.

Birthdays: Edwin Hubble, 1889; Alistair Cooke, 1908; Robert F. Kennedy, 1925; Richard Dawson, 1932; Dick Smothers, 1939; Joe Biden, 1942; Duane Allman, 1946; Joe Walsh, 1947; Bo Derek, 1956; Joel McHale, 1971; Dierks Bentley, 1975; Future, 1983

Trivia: What do a.m. and p.m. stand for, anyway?

Trivia Answer: "Ante meridiem", Latin for "before noon" and "post meridiem" for "after noon" – The custom of beginning days at midnight rather than at sunset comes to us from the Romans.

NOVEMBER

On This Date: On November 21, 1964, the world's longest suspension bridge opened over the Verrazano Narrows between Brooklyn and Staten Island.

Birthdays: Voltaire, 1694; Stan Musial, 1920; Marlo Thomas, 1937; Harold Ramis, 1944; Goldie Hawn, 1945; Nicollette Sheridan, 1963; Björk, 1965; Troy Aikman, 1966; Ken Griffey Jr., 1969; Michael Strahan, 1971; Jena Malone, 1984; Carly Rae Jepsen, 1985

Trivia: Which state has the longest coastline?

Trivia Answer: By far, it's Alaska. In fact, its coastline is longer than that of all the other coastal states combined! Strange that it never became a beach resort...

NOVEMBER

On This Date: On November 22, 1963, President John F. Kennedy was assassinated in a motorcade in Dallas, Texas.

Birthdays: Charles de Gaulle, 1890; Rodney Dangerfield, 1921; Terry Gilliam, 1940; Billie Jean King, 1943; Steven Van Zandt, 1950; Jamie Lee Curtis, 1958; Boris Becker, 1967; Mark Ruffalo, 1967; Scarlett Johansson, 1984; Oscar Pistorius, 1986

Trivia: Which president is credited with making Thanksgiving an official holiday?

Trivia Answer: Abe Lincoln proclaimed the last Thursday in November be celebrated back in 1863.

NOVEMBER

On This Date: On November 23, 1984, one of the most famous plays in football history took place when Doug Flutie's "Hail Mary" pass fell into the hands of receiver Gerard Phelan to give Boston College a dramatic 47-45 win over Miami.

Birthdays: Franklin Pierce, 1804; Boris Karloff, 1887; Harpo Marx, 1888; Robin Roberts, 1960; Daniel Snyder, 1964; Nicole "Snooki" Polizzi, 1987; Miley Cyrus, 1992

Trivia: How many players are on a cricket team?

Trivia Answer: 11

NOVEMBER

On This Date: On November 24, 1963, Kennedy assassin Lee Harvey Oswald was shot to death in Dallas, Texas, by Jack Ruby.

Birthdays: Zachary Taylor, 1784; William F. Buckley, Jr., 1925; Oscar Robertson, 1938; Paul Tagliabue, 1940; Pete Best, 1941; Ted Bundy, 1946; Rudy Tomjanovich, 1948; Stephen Merchant, 1974; Colin Hanks, 1977; Katherine Heigl, 1978

Trivia: What does GPS stand for?

Trivia Answer: Global Positioning System

NOVEMBER

On This Date: On November 25, 1952, Agatha Christie's *The Mousetrap* opened in London at the Ambassador Theater. More than 25,000 performances later, it is still running!

Birthdays: Andrew Carnegie, 1835; Joe DiMaggio, 1914; Ricardo Montalban, 1920; Joe Gibbs, 1940; Ben Stein, 1944; John Larroquette, 1947; Amy Grant, 1960; John F. Kennedy Jr., 1960; Cris Carter, 1965; Christina Applegate, 1971; Donovan McNabb, 1976; Barbara Pierce Bush & Jenna Bush Hager, 1981

Trivia: The life story of NFL offensive tackle Michael Oher provided the inspiration for what Best Picture nominee?

Trivia Answer: The Blind Side

NOVEMBER

On This Date: On November 26, 2003, the Concorde supersonic transport (SST), which featured a cruising speed of 1,350 miles per hour, made its final flight. Low passenger numbers and rising maintenance costs were among the factors for its retirement.

Birthdays: Charles Schulz; 1922; Robert Goulet, 1933; Rich Little, 1938; Tina Turner, 1939; Shawn Kemp, 1969; Natasha Bedingfield, 1981

Trivia: What is the color of the "black box" that serves as an airplane's voice recorder?

Trivia Answer: Orange

NOVEMBER

On This Date: On November 27, 1966, the defense rested. The Redskins outscored the Giants, 72-41, in a game that set the NFL record for total points.

Birthdays: Chick Hearn, 1916; Bruce Lee, 1940; Jimi Hendrix, 1942; Kathryn Bigelow, 1951; Bill Nye, 1955; Caroline Kennedy, 1957; Robin Givens, 1964; Jaleel White, 1976

Trivia: Along with Kyle Gass, who formed the satirical rock duo Tenacious D in the mid-1990s?

Trivia Answer: Jack Black

NOVEMBER

On This Date: On November 28, 1925, the Grand Ole Opry hit the airwaves with its first broadcast from WSM in Nashville.

Birthdays: William Blake, 1757; Berry Gordy, 1929; Randy Newman, 1943; Paul Shaffer, 1949; Ed Harris, 1950; Judd Nelson, 1959; Jon Stewart, 1962; Anna Nicole Smith, 1967; Chase Elliott, 1995

Trivia: The Singing Cowboy has the most stars on the Hollywood Walk of Fame, with five (for five different entertainment categories). Can you name him?

Trivia Answer: Gene Autry

NOVEMBER

On This Date: On November 29, 1947, the United Nations voted for the partition of Palestine and the creation of an independent Jewish state.

Birthdays: Louisa May Alcott, 1832; C.S. Lewis, 1898; Vin Scully, 1927; Garry Shandling, 1949; Joel Coen, 1954; Howie Mandel, 1955; Janet Napolitano, 1957; Rahm Emanuel, 1959; Don Cheadle, 1964; Mariano Rivera, 1969; Anna Faris, 1976; Russell Wilson, 1988

Trivia: This famous pop music group fashioned their four-letter name, beginning and ending with the same letter, after a Swedish fish-canning company.

Trivia Answer: Abba

NOVEMBER

On This Date: On November 30, 2004, after winning 74 straight games and more than $2.5 million– a record for U.S. game shows– *Jeopardy!* contestant Ken Jennings was finally defeated.

Birthdays: Jonathan Swift, 1667; Mark Twain, 1835; Winston Churchill, 1874; Dick Clark, 1929; G. Gordon Liddy, 1930; Bill Walsh, 1931; Abbie Hoffman, 1936; Ridley Scott, 1937; Mandy Patinkin, 1952; Billy Idol, 1955; Bo Jackson, 1962; Ben Stiller, 1965; Clay Aiken, 1978; Elisha Cuthbert, 1982; Kaley Cuoco, 1985; Chrissy Teigen, 1985

Trivia: In 2007, who replaced Bob Barker as the new host of *The Price Is Right*?

Trivia Answer: Drew Carey

DECEMBER

On This Date: On December 1, 1956, the Army made the decision to retire its last combat mule troop. Scuttlebutt has it that they just kicked them upstairs and they've been running the Pentagon ever since.

Birthdays: Lou Rawls, 1933; Woody Allen, 1935; Lee Trevino, 1939; Richard Pryor, 1940; Bette Midler, 1945; Pablo Escobar, 1949; Sarah Silverman, 1970; Janelle Monae, 1985

Trivia: Jaguars suffer from cynophobia, which is a fear of what kind of animal?

Trivia Answer: Dogs

DECEMBER

On This Date: On December 2, 1949, Gene Autry hit the record charts with his song *Rudolph, the Red-Nosed Reindeer.*

Birthdays: Harry Reid, 1939; Stone Phillips, 1954; Lucy Liu, 1968; Monica Seles, 1973; Jason Collins, 1978; Nelly Furtado, 1978; Britney Spears, 1981; Aaron Rodgers, 1983

Trivia: What is the only animal born with horns?

Trivia Answer: The giraffe

DECEMBER

On This Date: On December 3, 1967, a team led by Dr. Christian Barnard in South Africa performed the first successful human heart transplant. The patient survived 18 days before succumbing to complications.

Birthdays: George B. McClellan, 1826; Andy Williams, 1927; Ozzy Osbourne, 1948; Daryl Hannah, 1960; Julianne Moore, 1960; Brendan Fraser, 1968; Sean Parker, 1979; Andy Grammer, 1983; Amanda Seyfried, 1985

Trivia: Which heart beats faster: an elephant's or a canary's?

Trivia Answer: The canary's beats at a much heartier rate – 1,000 times a minute compared to the 25 times per minute of an elephant's heart.

DECEMBER

On This Date: On December 4, 1980, Polish track star Stella Walsh, the 1932 Olympic gold medalist in the 100-yard dash, died during an armed robbery at which "she" was an innocent bystander. After the autopsy in Cleveland, Ohio, the coroner announced that "she" was a "he."

Birthdays: Jeff Bridges, 1949; Marisa Tomei, 1964; Fred Armisen, 1966; Jay Z, 1969; Tyra Banks, 1973

Trivia: Fight announcer Michael Buffer has made more than 400 million dollars since he trademarked what catchphrase?

Trivia Answer: "Let's get ready to rumble!"

DECEMBER

On This Date: On December 5, 1933, happy days were here again as Prohibition formally ended with the repeal of the 18th Amendment by the 21st.

Birthdays: Martin Van Buren, 1782; George Custer, 1839; Walt Disney, 1901; Little Richard, 1932; Jim Tressel, 1952; John Rzeznik, 1965; Margaret Cho, 1968; Paula Patton, 1975; Frankie Muniz, 1985

Trivia: How many amendments are there in the current U.S. Constitution?

Trivia Answer: 27

DECEMBER

On This Date: On December 6, 1790, Congress moved from New York to Philadelphia. They soon wore out their welcome there as well, and kept going south to Washington, D.C.

Birthdays: Otto Graham, 1921; Steven Wright, 1955; Andrew Cuomo, 1957; Debbie Rowe, 1958; Judd Apatow, 1967; Johnny Manziel, 1992; Elian Gonzalez, 1993

Trivia: What is the world's northernmost capital?

Trivia Answer: Reykjavik, Iceland

DECEMBER

On This Date: On December 7, 1941, Japanese warplanes attacked Pearl Harbor, an act that led to America's entry into World War II.

Birthdays: Ted Knight, 1923; Noam Chomsky, 1928; Harry Chapin, 1942; Johnny Bench, 1947; Tom Waits, 1949; Larry Bird, 1956; C. Thomas Howell, 1966; Terrell Owens, 1973; Sara Bareilles, 1979; Aaron Carter, 1987; Yasiel Puig, 1990

Trivia: American soldiers have often been referred to as "G.I.s". What does G.I. stand for?

Trivia Answer: "General Issue", the term stamped on their clothing, equipment and supplies (In some quarters it is referred to as "Government Issue".)

DECEMBER

On This Date: On December 8, 1980, John
Lennon was gunned down in New York.

Birthdays: Diego Rivera, 1886; Sammy Davis Jr., 1925;
Flip Wilson, 1933; David Carradine, 1936; Jim Morrison, 1943;
Gregg Allman, 1947; Kim Basinger, 1953; Sam Kinison, 1953;
Ann Coulter, 1961; Teri Hatcher, 1964; Sinead O'Connor, 1966;
Philip Rivers, 1981; Nicki Minaj, 1982; Josh Donaldson, 1985;
Dwight Howard, 1985

Trivia: The Beatles' first American television appearance
was…?

Trivia Answer: On The Huntley-Brinkley Report, *with a news piece by Edwin Newman
in 1963*

DECEMBER

On This Date: On December 9, 1907, the
Wilmington, Delaware, post office sold the very
first Christmas seals.

Birthdays: Douglas Fairbanks Jr., 1909; Tip O'Neill, 1912;
Kirk Douglas, 1916; Redd Foxx, 1922; Judi Dench, 1934;
Deacon Jones, 1938; Beau Bridges, 1941; Dick Butkus, 1942;
John Malkovich, 1953; Donny Osmond, 1957; Felicity Huffman,
1962; Kara DioGuardi, 1970; McKayla Maroney, 1995

Trivia: Who is the only actor to win an Oscar for playing Santa
Claus?

*Trivia Answer: Edmund Gwenn – He won as Best Supporting Actor for his role as St.
Nick in* Miracle on 34th Street.

DECEMBER

On This Date: On December 10, 1799, France became the first country to adopt the metric system.

Birthdays: Emily Dickinson, 1830; Chet Huntley, 1911; Dorothy Lamour, 1914; Dan Blocker, 1928; Rod Blagojevich, 1956; Michael Clarke Duncan, 1957; Kenneth Branagh, 1960; Bobby Flay, 1964; Meg White, 1974; Raven-Symone, 1985

Trivia: How long is a fortnight?

Trivia Answer: Two weeks

DECEMBER

On This Date: On December 11, 1972, Apollo 17 made a lunar landing and three days later astronaut Eugene Cernan became the last man, to date, to set foot on the moon.

Birthdays: Rita Moreno, 1931; John Kerry, 1943; Brenda Lee, 1944; Jermaine Jackson, 1954; Mo'Nique, 1967; Mos Def, 1973

Trivia: How many millions are in a trillion?

Trivia Answer: One million (A thousand millions make a billion and one thousand billions make a trillion.)

DECEMBER

On This Date: On December 12, 1925, the world's first motel, the Motel Inn in San Luis Obispo, California, opened for business. It was designed by Arthur Heineman, who also coined the term "motel".

Birthdays: Frank Sinatra, 1915; Bob Barker, 1923; Ed Koch, 1924; Bob Pettit, 1932; Connie Francis, 1938; Dionne Warwick, 1940; Cathy Rigby, 1952; Jennifer Connelly, 1970; Mayim Bialik, 1975

Trivia: How many sides does a stop sign have?

Trivia Answer: 8- It's an octagon.

DECEMBER

On This Date: On December 13, 2003, former Iraqi President Saddam Hussein was captured. He would be executed three years later.

Birthdays: Mary Todd Lincoln, 1818; Larry Doby, 1923; Dick Van Dyke, 1925; John Davidson, 1941; Ted Nugent, 1948; Ben Bernanke, 1953; Steve Buscemi, 1957; Rex Ryan, 1962; Mike Tirico, 1966; Jamie Foxx, 1967; Sergei Federov, 1969; Amy Lee, 1981; Taylor Swift, 1989

Trivia: What is the only continent without a desert?

Trivia Answer: Europe

DECEMBER

On This Date: On December 14, 1799, George Washington died at Mount Vernon, Virginia, at the age of 67.

Birthdays: Nostradamus, 1503; Don Hewitt, 1922; Ernie Davis, 1939; Patty Duke, 1946; Bill Buckner, 1949; James Comey, 1960; Craig Biggio, 1965; Vanessa Hudgens, 1988

Trivia: What role did James Gandolfini play on *The Sopranos*?

Trivia Answer: Tony Soprano

DECEMBER

On This Date: On December 15, 1939, the world premiere of *Gone with the Wind* took place in Atlanta.

Birthdays: Gustave Eiffel, 1832; Tim Conway, 1933; Don Johnson, 1949; Rodney Harrison, 1972; Michelle Dockery, 1981; Josh Norman, 1987

Trivia: "Taste the rainbow" is the slogan of what candy?

Trivia Answer: Skittles

DECEMBER

16

On This Date: On December 16, 1773, colonists dressed as Indians and threw tea into Boston Harbor. You know it, of course, as the Boston Tea Party.

Birthdays: Ludwig van Beethoven, 1770; Jane Austen, 1775; Arthur C. Clarke, 1917; Lesley Stahl, 1941; Billy Gibbons, 1949; William "Refrigerator" Perry, 1962; Benjamin Bratt, 1963; J.B. Smoove, 1965; Donovan Bailey, 1967

Trivia: When Jeff Bezos founded this online company in 1994, it was called Cadabra.

Trivia Answer: Amazon.com

DECEMBER

17

On This Date: On December 17, 1903, Orville and Wilbur Wright made the first successful man-powered airplane flights, near Kitty Hawk, North Carolina. Orville piloted the 12-second inaugural flight, which covered 120 feet.

Birthdays: William Safire, 1929; Pope Francis, 1936; Chris Matthews, 1945; Eugene Levy, 1946; Bill Pullman, 1953; Chuck Liddell, 1969; Sarah Paulson, 1974; Milla Jovovich, 1975; Manny Pacquiao, 1978; Buddy Hield, 1993

Trivia: To the nearest mile, how long is a marathon?

Trivia Answer: 26 - 26.2, to be exact

DECEMBER 18

On This Date: On December 18, 1620, the Mayflower docked at Plymouth Harbor as its passengers began their new settlement.

Birthdays: Franz Ferdinand, 1863; Joseph Stalin, 1878; Ty Cobb, 1886; Betty Grable, 1916; Keith Richards, 1943; Steven Spielberg, 1946; Ray Liotta, 1954; Brad Pitt, 1963; "Stone Cold" Steve Austin, 1964; DMX, 1970; Sia Furler, 1975; Katie Holmes, 1978; Christina Aguilera, 1980

Trivia: What is the first day of the winter season called?

Trivia Answer: Winter Solstice

DECEMBER 19

On This Date: On December 19, 1732, *Poor Richard's Almanack* began publication in Philadelphia by Ben Franklin.

Birthdays: Little Jimmy Dickens, 1920; Phil Ochs, 1940; Maurice White, 1941; Robert Urich 1946; Kevin McHale, 1957; Reggie White, 1961; Jennifer Beals, 1963; Criss Angel, 1967; Tyson Beckford, 1970; Alyssa Milano 1972; Warren Sapp, 1972; Jake Gyllenhaal, 1980

Trivia: True or false? You can't copyright a book title.

Trivia Answer: True

DECEMBER

On This Date: On December 20, 1957, Elvis Presley received his draft notice to serve in the U.S. Army.

Birthdays: Harvey Firestone, 1868; Branch Rickey, 1881; Bob Hayes, 1942; Uri Geller, 1946; Dick Wolf, 1946; David Cook, 1982; David Wright, 1982; Jonah Hill, 1983; JoJo, 1990

Trivia: What has been perpetually guarded at Arlington National Cemetery by the U.S. Army since July of 1937?

Trivia Answer: The Tomb of the Unknowns

DECEMBER

On This Date: On December 21, 1937, *Snow White and the Seven Dwarfs* made its film premiere. At a later date at the Academy Awards, Walt Disney received a special Oscar for the movie- along with seven miniature ones.

Birthdays: Josh Gibson, 1911; Joe Paterno, 1926; Phil Donahue, 1935; Jane Fonda, 1937; Frank Zappa, 1940; Samuel L. Jackson, 1948; Chris Evert, 1954; Jane Kaczmarek, 1955; Ray Romano, 1957; Florence Griffith Joyner, 1959; Andy Dick, 1965; Kiefer Sutherland, 1966; Karrie Webb, 1974

Trivia: Only four words in the English language begin with "dw". One is "dwarf". What are the other three?

Trivia Answer: Dweeb, dwell and dwindle

DECEMBER

On This Date: On December 22, 1956, Colo entered the world at the Columbus Zoo in Ohio. Colo was the first-ever gorilla born in captivity.

Birthdays: Connie Mack, 1862; Claudia "Lady Bird" Johnson, 1912; Barbara Billingsley, 1915; Steve Carlton, 1944; Diane Sawyer, 1945; Maurice & Robin Gibb, 1949; Ralph Fiennes, 1962; Ted Cruz, 1970; Jordin Sparks, 1989; Meghan Trainor, 1993

Trivia: Do you know the only members of the animal kingdom to commonly sleep on their backs?

Trivia Answer: Human beings

DECEMBER

On This Date: On December 23, 1888, Dutch painter Vincent van Gogh, suffering from depression, cut off the lower part of his left ear with a razor while staying in Arles, France. He later documented the event in a painting titled *Self-Portrait with Bandaged Ear*.

Birthdays: Emperor Akihito, 1933; Paul Hornung, 1935; Harry Shearer, 1943; Susan Lucci, 1946; Jim Harbaugh, 1963; Eddie Vedder, 1964; Naked Cowboy, 1970; Corey Haim, 1971

Trivia: Aside from Mona Lisa's cryptic smile, what's unusual about her face?

Trivia Answer: She has no eyebrows.

DECEMBER 24

On This Date: On December 24, 1814, the War of 1812 ended when the U.S. and Great Britain signed the Treaty of Ghent.

Birthdays: Howard Hughes, 1905; Ava Gardner, 1922; Mary Higgins Clark 1927; Hamid Karzai, 1957; Lee Daniels, 1959; Diedrich Bader, 1966; Ricky Martin, 1971; Stephenie Meyer, 1973; Ryan Seacrest, 1974; Louis Tomlinson, 1991

Trivia: Which one of the reindeer is never mentioned in *The Night Before Christmas*?

Trivia Answer: Rudolph

DECEMBER 25

On This Date: On December 25, 1818, *Silent Night* was introduced to the world. And, of course, every year on this date, Santa sits back, kicks off his boots, props up his feet, sips hot cocoa and heaves a great sigh of relief!

Birthdays: Clara Barton, 1821; Robert Ripley, 1890; Humphrey Bogart, 1899; Anwar Sadat, 1918; Rod Serling, 1924; Nellie Fox, 1927; Ken Stabler, 1945; Jimmy Buffett, 1946; Larry Csonka, 1946; Barbara Mandrell, 1948; Sissy Spacek, 1949; Karl Rove, 1950; Annie Lennox, 1954; Rickey Henderson, 1958; Dido, 1971; Justin Trudeau, 1971; Demaryius Thomas, 1987

Trivia: Santa Claus is known as "Hoteiosho" in what land?

Trivia Answer: Japan

DECEMBER

On This Date: On December 26, 1865, James
Nason of Franklin, Massachusetts, received a patent for
the first coffee percolator.

Birthdays: George Dewey, 1837; Mao Tse-tung, 1893;
Steve Allen, 1921; Alan King, 1927; Phil Spector, 1939; Bill Ayers,
1944; John Walsh, 1945; Carlton Fisk, 1947; Ozzie Smith, 1954;
David Sedaris, 1956; Lars Ulrich, 1963; Jared Leto, 1971;
Chris Daughtry, 1979; Beth Behrs, 1985; Kit Harington, 1986

Trivia: What popular beverage was introduced in 1929 as
Bib-Label Lithiated Lemon-Lime Soda?

*Trivia Answer: Imagine having to write a jingle for that name! Fortunately the bottlers
wised up and rechristened the drink 7-Up.*

DECEMBER

On This Date: On December 27, 1932, Radio City
Music Hall opened in New York City.

Birthdays: Johannes Kepler, 1571; Louis Pasteur, 1822;
Marlene Dietrich, 1901; Chyna, 1969; Savannah Guthrie, 1971;
Heather O'Rourke, 1975; Carson Palmer, 1979

Trivia: Of culinary celebrities Betty Crocker, Aunt Jemima and
Mrs. Fields, which one is real?

Trivia Answer: Mrs. Fields- Debbi Fields founded the cookie company in 1977.

DECEMBER

On This Date: On December 28, 1958, the NFL Championship was decided in sudden death for the first time. The Colts scored a 23-17 win over the Giants in "The Greatest Game Ever Played."

Birthdays: Woodrow Wilson, 1856; Stan Lee, 1922; Terry Sawchuk, 1929; Nichelle Nichols, 1932; Gayle King, 1954; Denzel Washington, 1954; Ray Bourque, 1960; Adam Vinatieri, 1972; Seth Meyers, 1973; Joe Manganiello, 1976; John Legend, 1978; Sienna Miller, 1981

Trivia: Who's the model for the NBA's silhouette logo?

Trivia Answer: Jerry West

DECEMBER

On This Date: On December 29, 1845, Texas became the 28th state admitted to the United States of America.

Birthdays: Andrew Johnson, 1808; W.E. Gladstone, 1809; Mary Tyler Moore, 1936; Jon Voight, 1938; Marianne Faithfull, 1946; Ted Danson, 1947; Patricia Clarkson, 1959; Jude Law, 1972; Mekhi Phifer, 1974

Trivia: The moan of "I can't believe I ate the whole thing" turned everyone into a salesperson for this product.

Trivia Answer: Alka-Seltzer

DECEMBER

On This Date: On December 30, 1940, the six-lane Arroyo Seco Parkway, which connects downtown L.A. and Pasadena, opened. The California freeway is considered to be the first of its kind in the United States.

Birthdays: Rudyard Kipling, 1865; Bo Diddley, 1928; Sandy Koufax, 1935; Jim Marshall, 1937; Paul Stookey, 1937; Michael Nesmith, 1942; Davy Jones, 1945; Patti Smith, 1946; Meredith Vieira, 1953; Matt Lauer, 1957; Tracey Ullman, 1959; Tiger Woods, 1975; Laila Ali, 1977; Tyrese Gibson, 1978; Eliza Dushku, 1980; LeBron James, 1984; Ellie Goulding, 1986

Trivia: What TV personality was an on-screen love interest of future real-life husband Mark Consuelos on *All My Children*?

Trivia Answer: Kelly Ripa

DECEMBER

On This Date: On December 31, 1904, the first New Year's Eve celebration was held in Times Square (formerly known as Longacre Square), in New York.

Birthdays: Jacques Cartier, 1491; Anthony Hopkins, 1937; John Denver, 1943; Ben Kingsley, 1943; Donna Summer, 1948; Val Kilmer, 1959; Nicholas Sparks, 1965; Joey McIntyre, 1972; Psy, 1977; Gabby Douglas, 1995

Trivia: If you suffered from pogonophobia, you might be afraid of Santa Claus. Why?

Trivia Answer: Pogonophobia is a fear of beards.